THE SONGS OF BEN SIDRAN 1970-2020, Vol. 1

NARDIS

Music Prepared by Jeremy Borum / jeremyborum.com
Book Design by Jamie Breiwick, B Side Graphics / bsidegraphics.net
©2023 Unlimited Media, Ltd. / Nardis Books   ISBN: 9798218227630

THE SONGS OF BEN SIDRAN 1970-2020, Vol. 1

CONTENTS

Preface	4
A Is For Alligator	5
About Love	8
Ask Me Now	11
At Least We Got To The Race	14
Back Nine	16
Blue Camus	20
Brand New Music	22
Broad Daylight	24
Chances Are	26
Choice In The Matter	28
Critics	30
Don't Cry For No Hipster	34
Enivre d'Amour	38
Face Your Fears	40
Feel Your Groove	43
Free In America	47
Fullness Of Time	52
Get It Yourself	54
Get To The Point	58
Girl Talk	60
Have You Heard The News	64
I Might Be Wrong	67
I Wanna Be A Bebopper	71
In The Beginning	74
It Didn't All Come True	77
It Don't Get No Better	80
King Of Harlem	82
Let's Make A Deal	86
Life's A Lesson	89
Lip Service	94
Little Sherry	96
Midnight Tango	100
Minority	104
Mitsubishi Boy	106
Monk's Mood	110
Nardis	114
Old Hoagy	117
On The Cool Side	121
Piano Players	123
Picture Him Happy	129
Private Guy	132
Rich Interior Life	134
Searching For A Girl Like You	137
See You On The Other Side	141
She Steps Into A Dream	144
So Long	146
Solar	148
Song For A Sucker Like You	152
Take A Little Hit	156
Thank God For The F Train	158
There They Go	161
Too Hot To Touch	165
Too Much Too Late	168
Turn To The Music	173
Walking With The Blues	177
Who's The Old Guy Now	180

Other Books by Ben Sidran	183
Credits	184

PREFACE

Jazz musicians call these music pages "charts" or "road maps" because they are designed to be a spiritual and literal GPS for the exploration of a musical premise. Hence, a song. They provide a starting point and a destination and along the route, one is free to get waylaid under the stars or drift on the high seas. One can (metaphorically) climb the trees and swing from the branches. The object in any case is to swing. To play these charts one should probably learn to sing the songs first because the words and the music are the same; at least they support one another and have a mutual purpose. I consider myself a spoken-word performer as much as a singer, so some melodies are written out and some are left open (slashes instead of notes) to encourage freedom in interpretation. After all, I'm making a lot of it up as I go. So the trip is the performance, and these pages are the maps.

– **Ben Sidran, February 2023**

Photo credit Nathan Cox

A IS FOR ALLIGATOR

BEN & LEO SIDRAN

MAYBE THERE'S A WAY TO LET THE ALLIGATOR PLAY INSIDE THE BATHTUB
MAYBE THERE'S A WAY THAT WE CAN PLAY INSIDE THE BATHTUB TOO
MAYBE THERE'S A SONG THAT YOU AND I CAN SING ALONG ABOUT THE BATHTUB
BUT IF THERE IS IT'S JUST A SONG ABOUT THE DAY THAT WE WERE ALLIGATORS TOO

ONCE THERE WAS A TIME WHEN ALL THE ANIMALS WOULD CLIMB INSIDE THE BATHTUB
THE MONKEY AND THE LION AND THE ZEBRA AND THE ALLIGATOR TOO
ONCE THERE WAS A GAME THAT ALL THE ANIMALS WOULD PLAY INSIDE THE BATHTUB
BUT NOW THE ONLY GAME WE PLAY IS YOU EAT ME OR BABY I'LL EAT YOU

MAYBE THAT'S THE REASON PEOPLE FINALLY HAD TO BUILD THEMSELVES A ZOO
THEY CALL IT NEW YORK CITY BUT IT'S JUST ANOTHER ALLIGATOR STEW

NOW YOU AND I ARE ALLIGATORS TOO
YOU AND I ARE ALLIGATORS TOO

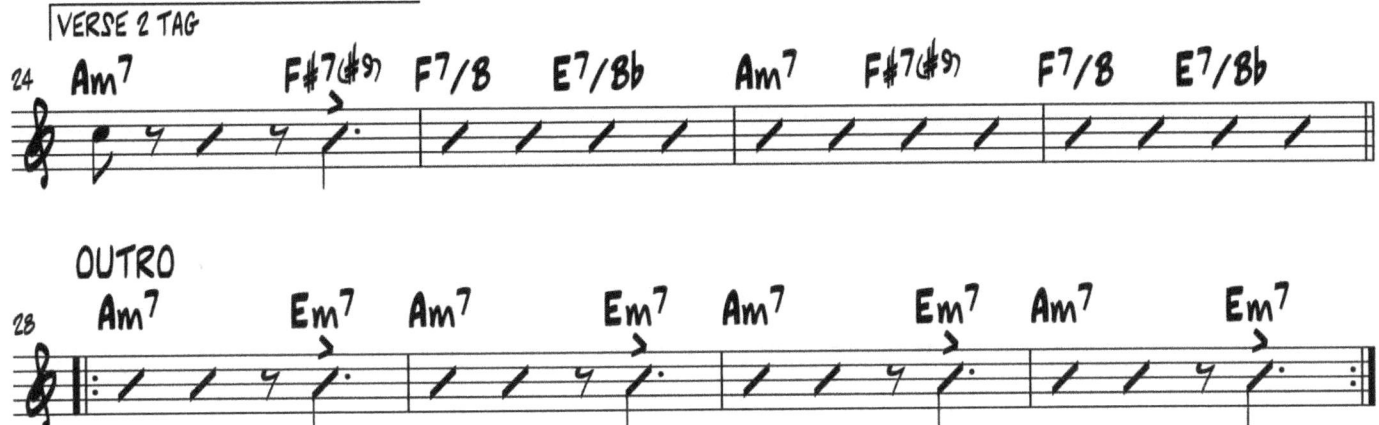

ABOUT LOVE

BEN SIDRAN

I GOT SOME NEWS FOR YOU DARLING AND IT GOES LIKE THIS
I GOT MY EYES WIDE OPEN NOT A THING I MISSED
I GOT SOME NEWS
NEWS FOR YOU DEAR
WELL I KNOW YOU LOOK SO FINE
BUT DON'T YOU TRY THAT PARTY LINE AROUND HERE
MY LADY FAIR
DON'T YOU CARE
NOT AT ALL
ABOUT LOVE
ABOUT LOVE

I GOT SOME NEWS SLIPPERY SISTER AND IT GOES LIKE THIS
I GOT MY EYES WIDE OPEN NOT A THING I MISSED
I GOT SOME NEWS, NEWS FOR YOU DEAR
WELL YOU SPREAD YOURSELF SO THIN
I'M GONNA HAVE TO TAKE YOU IN
AND KEEP YOU HERE
MY LADY FAIR
DON'T YOU CARE
NOT AT ALL
ABOUT LOVE
ABOUT LOVE

1971, Recording in the famed Studio A at Capitol Records; the band included two drummers (Jim Keltner and Gary Mallaber) and guitarist Jesse "Ed" Davis.

ASK ME NOW

THELONIOUS MONK
LYRICS BY BEN SIDRAN

OUR FRIENDS THEY TALK ABOUT US
THEIR LIVES GO ON WITHOUT US
THEY'RE LEAVING US TO END SOMEHOW
LOOKING AT THIS MESS DEAR
ANYBODY COULD GUESS DEAR
IF YOU'VE GOT QUESTIONS AS ME NOW
COME ON AND ASK ME
WHY DON'T YOU ASK ME

AND OUR WEEKEND CONVERSATIONS
HOLD FEW REVELATIONS
IT'S JUST TABLE TALK, IT'S CHAT THAT'S ALL
LET'S STOP PLAYING DUMB DEAR
INSTEAD OF COUNTING THESE CRUMBS DEAR
IF YOU'VE GOT QUESTIONS ASK ME NOW

WHY WAIT THROUGH ANOTHER MOVIE
JUST TO SAY, "HEY, LIFE AIN'T LIKE THAT"
HOLLYWOOD IT'S ALWAYS GROOVY
YEAH, THE PLASTIC IS FANTASTIC
BUT REAL LIFE JUST DON'T ROLL LIKE THAT

NOW YOU'RE ACTING STOIC
ME I FEEL HEROIC
BUT LIFE DEFEATS US ANYHOW
WHILE WE HIDE THIS PAIN DEAR
WE'RE STANDING IN THE RAIN DEAR
IF YOU'VE GOT QUESTIONS ASK ME NOW
LET THE TRUTH BE YOUR UMBRELLA
IF YOU'VE GOT QUESTIONS ASK ME NOW
HEY, COME ON AND ASK ME

NOW YOU'RE ACTING STOIC
ME I FEEL HEROIC
BUT LIFE DEFEATS US ANYHOW
LET'S PART LIKE WE MET DEAR
LET'S DO WITHOUT REGRETS DEAR
IF YOU'VE GOT QUESTIONS ASK ME NOW
SING YOUR SONG AND TAKE YOUR BOW
IF YOU'VE GOT QUESTIONS ASK ME NOW

ASK ME NOW

NOW YOU'RE ACTING STOIC...

D OUTRO VAMP

AT LEAST WE GOT TO THE RACE

BEN SIDRAN

AT LEAST WE GOT TO THE RACE
AT LEAST WE GOT TO THE PLACE WHERE YOU SHOW YOUR FACE
WE DIDN'T WIN WE DIDN'T SHOW WE DIDN'T PLACE
BUT AT LEAST WE GOT TO THE RACE

AT LEAST WE GOT TO THE BALL
WE MAYBE STUMBLED BUT WE DIDN'T TAKE A FALL
NO GLASS SLIPPERS, NO SHOES AT ALL
BUT AT LEAST WE GOT TO THE BALL

NOBODY COUNTED, COUNTED US IN
NOBODY THOUGHT THAT WE'D EVER WIN
THEY WERE RIGHT, RIGHT AFTER ALL
BUT WHILE THEY WERE COUNTING, WE HAD A BALL

AT LEAST WE MADE THE PARADE
AND WE WERE THERE WHEN THE PAYBACK WAS FINALLY PAID
WARM IN THE SUN, COOL IN THE SHADE
AT LEAST WE MADE THE PARADE

SAW LOTS OF OTHERS, SISTERS AND BROTHERS
LAY DOWN THEIR LOAD BY THE SIDE OF THE ROAD
BUT WHAT DID WE CARE WE JUST STAYED LAISSEZ FAIR
YOU CAN'T GET ENOUGH OF AFFIRMATIVE STUFF

AT LEAST WE FOUND OUR WAY HOME
DIDN'T HURT NOBODY, DIDN'T DO NOBODY WRONG
COULDN'T FIND THE SHORT WAY SO WE TOOK THE LONG
TO THE STROLL ROCK AND ROLL TO THE RACE DIG YOUR FACE
TO THE FAIR TO THE ZOO TO THE GAME ME AND YOU
AT LEAST WE FOUND OUR WAY HOME

BACK NINE

Ben & Leo Sidran

I MADE MY WAY TO THE BACK NINE
THEY CALL ME THE IRON MAN
WATCHING OUT FOR THE SAND TRAPS
FORMULATING MY PLAN
OUT ON THE BACK NINE
I KNOW HOW TO DO MY THING
I TRADED IN THE FIVE SPOT
FOR A NEW KIND OF CLUB
BUT I STILL MAINTAIN MY SWING
LIFE AIN'T NOTHING BUT FINE
OUT ON THE BACK NINE

LAYING BACK ON THE BACK NINE
THE HUSTLE IS STILL MY THING
DRIVE FOR SHOW, IN THE WHOLE FOR DOUGH
YOU KNOW THEY CALL ME THE RHYTHM KING
ON THE BACK NINE
IT'S A HAZARD JUST TO BE ALIVE
STILL HAVING FUN WITH THE OLD PITCH AND RUN
BUT NOW THE SCORE AIN'T NOTHING BUT JIVE
I GOT THE BIRD ON MY MIND
OUT ON THE BACK NINE

THINGS ARE GOOD ON THE BACK NINE
GOT THE VIEW FROM THE CLUB HOUSE TURN
RUNNING THE CHANGES ON THE DRIVING RANGES
WAITING FOR THE GRASS TO BURN
ON THE BACK NINE
EVERYTHING IS BY THE BOOK
GOT THE CADDY FOR DADDY
THE GLIDE IN MY STRIDE
JUST DEALING WITH A DIFFERENT HOOK
LIFE AIN'T NOTHING BUT FINE
OUT ON THE BACK NINE

BACK NINE

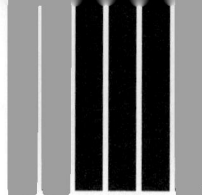

BACK NINE

I owe this song in part to the great British musician Georgie Fame. He loved the game of golf and Leo was thinking of him when he wrote the first verse to this song. The idea of being on the back nine is of course a metaphor for life, being closer to the end than one is to the beginning, aging with a natural swing and a love for playing the game. I wrote the additional verses using a series of puns comparing jazz with golf. Not surprisingly, considering all the aging golfers out there, this song became quite popular on jazz radio. That also might tell us something about jazz radio.

BLUE CAMUS

BEN & LEO SIDRAN

(SPOKEN WORD)

DOWN ON THE D'ORSAY SIDE WHERE THE RIVER'S JUST A MUDDY SLIDE
THERE'S A LITTLE SLIPAWAY WHERE THE ALGERIAN HIDES
UN HOMME DU MIDI, UN HOMME DÉTRUIT
UN HOMME DE LA VIE, C'EST TOUT C'EST FINI
SAY YOU WON'T LIVE YOUR LIFE IF YOU SPEND YOUR LIFE SEARCHING FOR THE KEY
IT'S JUST A PASSAGE IN THE SHADOWS BETWEEN WHAT'S WRONG AND WHAT'S RIGHT
WHERE IT GETS SO DARK YOU CAN'T EVEN SEE THE LIGHT
LA LUMIÈRE LA LUMIÈRE
JE PEUX PAS VOIR, JE PEUX PAS SENTIR
IT'S ALL SO DARK BUT BABY IT'S ALL IS SO CLEAR:

IF YOU DON'T SAY WHAT YOU WANT, WANT WHAT YOU SAY
YOU JUST HANGING IN THE CUT BETWEEN AVANT AND PASSE

TO THE OTHER GUY YOU'RE THE OTHER GUY
TO THE STRANGER YOU'RE THE STRANGER

IT GETS SO DARK YOU CAN'T EVEN SEE THE LIGHT
AND THERE'S A DANCE THAT YOU CAN DO BETWEEN THE DAY AND THE NIGHT
UN HOMME DU MIDI, UN HOMME DÉTRUIT
UN HOMME DE LA VIE, C'EST TOUT C'EST FINI
SAY YOU WON'T LIVE YOUR LIFE IF YOU'RE LOOKING FOR THE KEY
IF YOU SPEND YOUR LIFE LOOKING FOR THE WAY YOU'LL NEVER DO TOMORROW
WHAT YOU WON'T DO TODAY ENOUGH IS NEVER ENOUGH
WHEN TIME IS SLIPSLIDING AWAY
JE PEUX PAS VOIR, JE PEUX PAS SENTIR
IT'S ALL SO DARK BUT IT'S ALL SO CLEAR:

TO THE OTHER GUY YOU ARE THE OTHER GUY
TO THE STRANGER YOU'RE THE STRANGER

TO THE OTHER GUY YOU ARE THE OTHER GUY

BLUE CAMUS

BRAND NEW MUSIC

BEN SIDRAN

(SPOKEN WORD)

HEY, HOW'S THAT CAR WORKING OUT FOR YOU?
I HEAR YOU GOT IT IN BABY BLUE
GOT ALL THE GIRLS HOOGLIN' AFTER YOU
BUT SO ARE THE GANGSTERS AND THE POLICE TOO
WITH A CAR LIKE THAT
WHAT COULD POSSIBLY GO WRONG?
BRAND NEW MUSIC, SAME OLD SONG

SAY HOW'S THAT NEW JOB WORKING OUT FOR YOU?
YOU BUYING MONEY AND SELLING MONEY TOO
GOT ALL THE CATS HOOGLIN' AFTER YOU
JUST A MATTER OF TIME BEFORE ALL YOUR DREAMS COME TRUE
WITH A JOB LIKE THAT
WHAT COULD POSSIBLY GO WRONG?
BRAND NEW MUSIC, SAME OLD SONG

SAY HOW'S THAT NEW GIRL WORKING OUT FOR YOU?
SHE'S LONG AND TALL, SHE'S NASTY TOO
GOT ALL THE GUYS JUST HOOGLIN' AFTER YOU
YOU MIGHT NOT KNOW THIS BUT
SHE'S MY OLD LADY TOO
BUT HEY
WITH A GIRL LIKE THAT
WHAT COULD POSSIBLY GO WRONG?
BRAND NEW MUSIC
SAME OLD SONG

SAY HOW'RE THOSE NEW FRIENDS WORKING OUT FOR YOU?
YOU GOT LAWYERS, BANKERS, POLITICIANS TOO
THEY KNOW HOW TO PARTY THAT MUCH IS TRUE
NOTHING BUT SMOKE AND ASHES WHEN THOSE BOYS ARE THROUGH
WITH FRIENDS LIKE THAT WHAT COULD POSSIBLY GO WRONG?
BRAND NEW MUSIC, SAME OLD SONG

BROAD DAYLIGHT

BEN SIDRAN

I GOT TO THINKING ABOUT THAT GIRL LAST NIGHT
ABOUT HOW SHE KISSES ME AND HOLDS ME TIGHT
SHE DOES ME GOOD BUT WHY WON'T SHE DO ME RIGHT
I'M NOT COMPLAINING AND I DON'T WANNA FIGHT
YOU ARE THE ONLY GIRL FOR ME BUT GIRL
YOU ONLY WANT TO SEE ME AT NIGHT
WHAT'S WRONG WITH GETTING IT IN THE BROAD DAYLIGHT

FOR EXAMPLE I SAID "BABY HOW ABOUT SOME AFTERNOON DELIGHT"
YOU SAID, "I'D LIKE TO BUT MY SCHEDULE IS A LITTLE TIGHT
BUT HOW ABOUT LATER, 'ROUND ABOUT MIDNIGHT OR ONE"
I'M NOT COMPLAINING I'M JUST TALKING ABOUT FUN
YOU ARE THE ONLY GIRL FOR ME BUT GIRL
YOU ONLY WANT TO SEE ME AT NIGHT
WHAT'S WRONG WITH DOING IT IN THE BROAD DAYLIGHT

WHEN THE CURTAIN FALLS
AND WHEN THE NIGHT OWL CALLS
THEN YOU AND I CAN BE THE BEST OF FRIENDS
BUT AT THE BREAK OF DAY
GIRL YOU TURN YOUR FACE AWAY
AND THAT'S WHEN ALL OF THE GOOD TIMES END
YOU ARE THE ONLY GIRL FOR ME BUT GIRL
YOU ONLY WANT TO SEE ME AT NIGHT
WHAT'S WRONG WITH DOING IT IN THE BROAD DAYLIGHT

YOUR GOOD LOVE GIVES ME SUCH A THRILL
GETS ME HOT DOWN IN A SPOT TILL I CAN NOT SIT STILL
BUT WHEN YOU PUT THE FIRE OUT WHY YOU WANNA SHOUT
"OH LOOK AT THE TIME"
AND THEN YOU'RE GONE BEFORE THE SUN CAN SHINE
YOU ARE THE ONLY GIRL FOR ME BUT GIRL
YOU ONLY WANT TO SEE ME AT NIGHT
WHAT'S WRONG WITH DOING IT IN THE BROAD DAYLIGHT

WAS IT SOMETHING I SAID OR SOMETHING I DIDN'T SAY

CHANCES ARE

BEN SIDRAN

YOU'RE MY MAN
YOU GOT NO PLAN, GOT NO LEADS
YOU'RE JUST SEWING SEEDS
CHASING DREAMS
SO IT SEEMS THAT
CHANCES ARE,
YOU'VE GOT TO RUN AWAY
RUN AWAY
CHANCES ARE, CHANCES ARE

I LIKE YOUR FACE
GOT NO STYLE, GOT NO GRACE
BUT IN THEIR PLACE
YOU GOT HEART
AND THAT'S YOUR START TO MOVE

THEY DON'T CARE WHAT YOU DO
AS LONG AS THEY APPROVE
THEY DON'T CARE WHAT YOU'VE BEEN THROUGH
THEY DON'T CARE IF YOU
HANG WITH THE OTHERS OR
STAND BY YOUR BROTHERS
THE CHOICE IS YOURS
THE CHOICE IS YOURS

FIND YOUR GROOVE
AND NOW AND THEN BRING A FRIEND
AND IF YOU'RE IN NEED, SIMPLY SEND
A SINGLE WORD OF LOVE
CHANCES ARE
YOU'VE GOT TO RUN AWAY
RUN AWAY...

CHOICE IN THE MATTER

BEN SIDRAN

(MELODICALLY SPOKEN WORD)

MY BABY LEFT ME A LITTLE WHILE AGO
OF COURSE I TRIED TO STOP HER LIKE I DID SO MANY TIMES BEFORE
BUT THIS TIME SHE'S GONE FOR GOOD AIN'T COMING BACK NO MORE
HEY BABY IF YOU'RE IN THE SOUND OF MY VOICE
BELIEVE ME WHEN I TELL YOU I JUST DIDN'T HAVE ANY CHOICE IN THE MATTER
AS A MATTER OF FACT

SEE SHE WALKED UP TO ME AND SHE ASKED ME FOR A DIME
I THOUGHT SHE WANTED TO MAKE A PHONE CALL MAYBE CHECK THE CORRECT TIME
THE NEXT THING I KNOW SHE PUT HER HAND IN MY POCKET
THEN YOU COME AROUND THE CORNER SAY "YOU HAVING A GOOD TIME"
HEY BABY IF YOU'RE IN THE SOUND OF MY VOICE
BELIEVE ME WHEN I TELL YOU I JUST DIDN'T HAVE ANY CHOICE IN THE MATTER

AS A MATTER OF FACT
I DIDN'T EVEN DIG THE GIRL
I WAS JUST PLAYING AROUND WITH THE ACT
I WAS SUSPICIOUS OUT FRONT
I WAS SUSPICIOUS OUT BACK
AND NOW YOU SAY YOU YOU'RE THE ONE WHO'S SUSPICIOUS
WHAT KIND OF WAY IS THAT TO ACT

OK I KNOW IT LOOKED FUNNY FROM AN OUTSIDE POINT OF VIEW
AND THE FACT THAT I WAS ZIPPING UP NOW THAT MIGHT BE CONFUSING TOO
BUT YOU SAW ME TRYING TO SPLIT DON'T THAT GIVE YOU CLUE
I'M JUST A VICTIM OF CIRCUMSTANCE TRYING TO BRING IT HOME TO YOU
HEY BABY IF YOU'RE IN THE SOUND OF MY VOICE
BELIEVE ME WHEN I TELL YOU I JUST DIDN'T HAVE ANY CHOICE

OH, SHE'S NEVER GONNA BUY THAT
BUT WHAT CAN YOU DO WHEN THE TRUTH IS STRANGER THAN THE FACT
IT'S A HARD WORLD AND BEFORE YOU CALL YOUR MAN A LIER
LOOK OVER YOUR SHOULDER SEE YOUR OWN BACON SHAKIN' IN THE FIRE

CHOICE IN THE MATTER

CRITICS

BEN SIDRAN

(MELODICALLY SPOKEN WORD)

CHORUS:
CRITICS CAN'T EVEN FLOAT
THEY JUST STAND ON THE SHORE, WAVE AT THE BOAT

I ONCE KNEW A CRITIC BLIND AS HE COULD BE
HE COULD TASTE THE SALT, HE COULD HEAR THE SURF, HE COULDN'T EVEN FIND THE SEA
HE WAS CONVINCED OF HIS WISDOM, HE WAS UNFETTERED WITH THE FACTS
HE FINALLY SOLVED HIS PROBLEM, HE TOOK THE OCEAN OFF OF HIS MAPS
THAT'S RIGHT, HE TOOK THE OCEAN OF HIS MAPS. WHY'S THAT?

(CHORUS)

NOBODY'D PAY A QUARTER TO HEAR THAT CRITIC SING
IF YOU HUNG HIM FROM A GOOD HOOK, COULDN'T EVEN SWING
THEY NEVER PAY THE COVER, THEY NEVER BUY THE DRINK
BUT THEY HANG AROUND FOR HOURS JUST TO TELL YOU WHAT THEY THINK. WHY'S THAT?

(CHORUS)

THEY DID IT TO CHARLIE PARKER, THEY SAID HE WAS PLAYING JUNK
THEY DID IT TO TRANE, THEY DID IT TO MILES, THEY SAVED THE BEST FOR MONK
THEY DID IT TO PEPPER ADAMS, BROKE HIS HEART ALRIGHT
NOW CALL UP YOUR LOCAL CRITIC, SEE WHERE PEPPER IS PLAYING TONIGHT

(CHORUS)

SO WHEN YOU MEET THAT CRITIC FACE TO FACE, IF HE'S GOT ONE
OR TWO, OR THREE, OR SEVERAL ALL OVER THE PLACE
I KNOW YOU MIGHT BE TEMPTED TO REARRANGE HIS HEAD
JUST BECAUSE HE TOOK YOUR DOUGH AND BAKED IT IN HIS BREAD
BUT REMEMBER BROTHERS AND SISTERS HE'S LIVING HERE IN SIN
HE'S GETTING FAT ON YOU THIS TIME BUT NEXT TIME, HE'S COMING BACK THIN

AS A SNAKE, A SNAKE NAMED JAKE ON THE TAKE. WHO'S THAT?

(CHORUS)

CRITICS

Ben Sidran

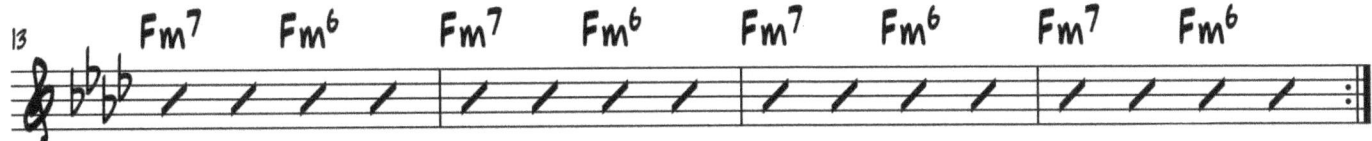

Lyrics:
- I ONCE KNEW A CRITIC...
- NOBODY'D PAY A QUARTER...
- THEY DID IT TO CHARLIE PARKER...
- SO WHEN YOU MEET THAT CRITIC...

CRITICS

This song came together on the last day of recording the album *Too Hot to Touch*. It was the spring of 1988 and we were in Minneapolis. That morning, I had been telling drummer Gordy Knudtson about a conversation I had had with the great saxophone player Pepper Adams just before he died. Pepper had been telling me about how the critics savaged him throughout his career, and, especially, how the critic John S. Wilson had singled him out for criticism after a concert he played with Thelonious Monk at Town Hall. Pepper actually took out his wallet and pulled a wrinkled piece of newspaper from the inside: it was a clipping of the actual review from years before. Pepper was still despondent over the fact that he felt this one bad review, not only of his playing but of the Monk project in general, had cost him the opportunity to work with Monk again (a six-week tour had been canceled). I told Gordy I was thinking of writing a song about critics, those reviewers who found it necessary to put a musician down in order to raise themselves up. I even had the hook: "Critics, they can't even float, they just stand on the shore and wave at the boat." Gordy said, "Let's do it. Right now." And so fifteen minutes later, he and bassist Billy Peterson were in the room throwing down a devolved (i.e. primitive) groove and I was in the lounge completing the lyrics.

with Gordy Knudtson, Bob Malach, Billy Peterson and Leo Sidran. Japan, 1987.

DON'T CRY FOR NO HIPSTER

BEN SIDRAN

DON'T CRY FOR NO HIPSTER
HE KNEW WHAT HE SIGNED UP FOR
THE LOOK AND THE FEEL
THAT RUN DOWN APPEAL
THE PASSING SHIP
THE DISTANT SHORE

DON'T CRY FOR NO HIPSTER
HE SAW THE WRITING ON THE WALL
IT STILL GIVES HIM HOPE
ANOTHER SLIPPERY SLOPE
A DEEPER TRUTH
HE CAN'T RECALL

BUT WHEN YOUNG BECOMES OLD
AND COOL TURNS TO COLD
THAT'S WHEN WE'LL SEE
IF THAT TRUTH SET HIM FREE

UNTIL THEN
DON'T CRY FOR NO HIPSTER
HE HAD HIS DAY HE HAD HIS NIGHT
CALL IT WHAT IT IS
IN A LIFE LIKE HIS
IT'S USUALLY WRONGS THAT MAKE IT RIGHT

HE'LL TELL YOU "I'M TIRED OF BEING SO HIP
IT'S LIKE WAITING FOR THAT SHIP
THAT DON'T NEVER COME IN, "
BUT CHECK OUT THE GRIN.

NO DON'T CRY FOR HIM,
DON'T CRY FOR NO HIPSTER
HE'S GOT HIS HAT HE'S GOT HIS CANE
IN A WORLD THIS SQUARE
DISASTERS EVERYWHERE
IF YOU CAN'T LAUGH AT LIFE YOU'RE THROUGH
BUT IF YOU HAVE TO CRY
IF YOU HAVE TO CRY THEN MAKE IT TEARS OF JOY
BECAUSE WE'RE HERE AND THEN WE'RE GONE
AND GONE IS ONE THING HE CAN DO.

DON'T CRY FOR NO HIPSTER

BEN SIDRAN

DON'T CRY FOR NO HIPSTER

This is me looking for me. This hipster has nothing to do with the fashion that emerged out of Brooklyn in the 21st century. Rather, the idea of a hipster goes all the way back to the American prohibition of the 1920's, when one entered a club with a hip flask full of one's favorite libation; that person was "hip". Later, jazz musicians extended the concept to someone who was "in the know, on the scene". In short, a jazz fan. Hipness was a kind of authenticity, of living the jazz life, that nitty-gritty "down at the heels" appeal. Saxophonist Phil Woods characterized it as "being a jazz warrior down to your socks.". Dave Frishberg famously lampooned people who pretended to be hip in his song "I'm Hip". I just saw it as a deep personal commitment to discovering if "the truth really sets you free" – experiencing everyday life on the ground level, true to your nature and that of your circumstance.

ENIVRE D'AMOUR

BEN SIDRAN

(SPOKEN WORD)

THE TRAIN FROM BERLIN SMOOTHES INTO THE GARDE DU NORD
WITH ITS PRECIOUS CARGO OF THE TERMINALLY BORED
THE TAXI IS FAST, THE COLORS RUN IN THE RAIN
THE CLUB IS THE BISTRO FOR THE SOCIALLY INSANE
YOU WANT TO KNOW ABOUT THE FIRE, GO WHERE THE FIRE IS
YOU WANT TO LEARN ABOUT LOVE BABY LEARN ABOUT THIS
ENIVRE D'AMOUR...
JE VEUX MOURIR IVRE D'AMOUR

THE FIRST THING YOU NOTICE IS THE SMELL OF HER PERFUME
A LITTLE FLUTTER OF WINGS WHEN SHE WALKS INTO THE ROOM
IT'S A DELICATE CUT, LIKE A KISS ON THE CHEEK
LIKE PASTIS ON ICE, IT'S A PRACTICE TRAGIQUE
BEAUTY IS IN THE EYE OF THE BEHOLDER IT'S TRUE
GONNA TURN OUT ALL THE LIGHTS, GONNA SEE THE REAL YOU
ENIVRE D'AMOUR...
JE VEUX MOURIR IVRE D'AMOUR

DENOUMENT, A MAGENTA SMUDGE ON A GLASS
AND THE WHISPER OF A TAXI MONTPARNASSE
LAST TANGO IN PARIS, LAST CALL FOR BERLIN
IT'S A PLAY YOU CAN MAKE, IT'S A PLAY YOU'LL NEVER WIN
YOU WANT TO LEARN ABOUT THE FIRE, GO WHERE THE FIRE IS
YOU WANT TO LEARN ABOUT LOVE BABY LEARN ABOUT THIS
ENIVRE D'AMOUR...
JE VEUX MOURIR IVRE D'AMOUR

COPYRIGHT © 1988 BEN SIDRAN
ADMINISTERED BY BULLDOG MUSIC. ALL RIGHTS RESERVED.

ENIVRE D'AMOUR

BEN SIDRAN

INTRO, STRAIGHT 8THS ♩ = 122

[Fm9] — 3X

A **VERSE** [Fm9]

THE TRAIN FROM BERLIN...
THE FIRST THING YOU NOTICE...
DENOUMENT, A MAGENTA SMUDGE...

[Bbm9] [Fm9]

[Bbm] [Gm7(b5)]

[Cm7(b13)] [Fm9]

B **BRIDGE**

[F#m9] [Amaj7/B] [F#m9] [Amaj7/B]

[Em9] [A9sus] [Em9] [C7(#9/b5)]

C [Fm7] [G/F] [Gb/F] [Fm]

[Fm7] [G/F] [Gb/F] [Fm]

COPYRIGHT © 1988 BEN SIDRAN
ADMINISTERED BY BULLDOG MUSIC. ALL RIGHTS RESERVED.

FACE YOUR FEARS

BEN SIDRAN

FACE YOUR FEARS
YOU GOT NOTHING TO LOSE BUT YOUR YEARS
FACE YOUR FEARS
YOU GOT NOTHING TO SHED BUT YOUR TEARS
MY DEAR
YOU'RE NOT YOUNG YOU'RE NOT OLD
YOU'RE JUST HERE

FACE YOUR FEARS
AND AS THE SILENCE OF NIGHT IT DRAWS NEAR
FACE YOUR FEARS
LIKE A BEACON OF LIGHT IT'S CLEAR
MY DEAR
YOU'RE NOT OLD
AND THERE IS NOTHING IN LIFE YOU SHOULD RUN FROM

FACE YOUR FEARS

BEN SIDRAN

FACE YOUR FEARS

In some sense, every song is written from the personal point of view. Yet when I asked Mose Allison if his songs were autobiographical, he said, "If I could live that life, I wouldn't need to write those songs." This song was written for my older sister who was going through a hard time. But the truth is life is difficult and we are all going through a hard time. Why this is so is one of the great mysteries of life. But this song suggests there is something one can do about it. If songs can be true, I hope this one is.

FEEL YOUR GROOVE

BEN SIDRAN

YES IT'S ME
AND I'M IN LOVE AGAIN
AIN'T FELT THIS WAY
SINCE I DON'T KNOW WHEN
AH BUT BABY
EVERY NOW AND THEN
I CAN REALLY FEEL YOUR GROOVE

YES IT'S ME
AND I'M HERE TO SAY
YOU, YOU'RE THE REASON
I FEEL THIS WAY
THE WAY YOU MOVE IT
THE WAY YOU LET IT LAY
I CAN REALLY FEEL YOUR GROOVE

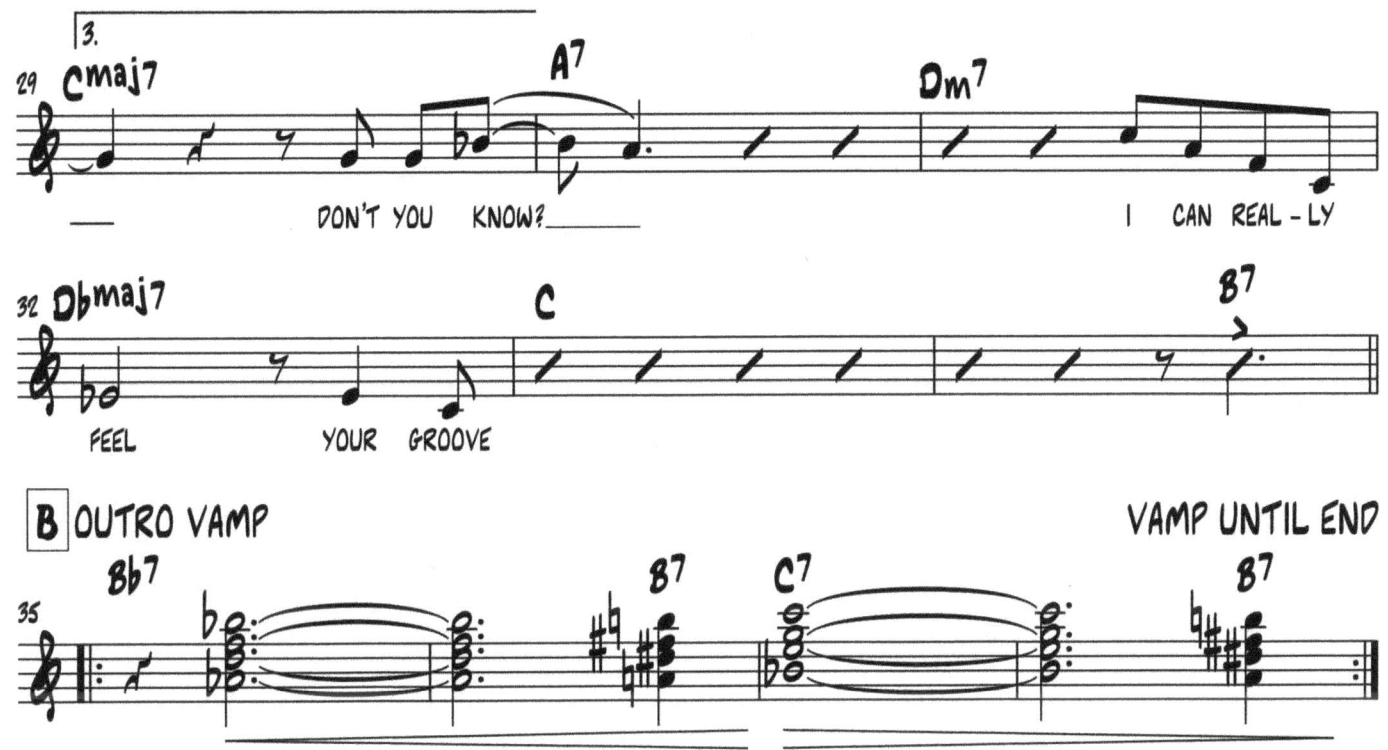

FEEL YOUR GROOVE

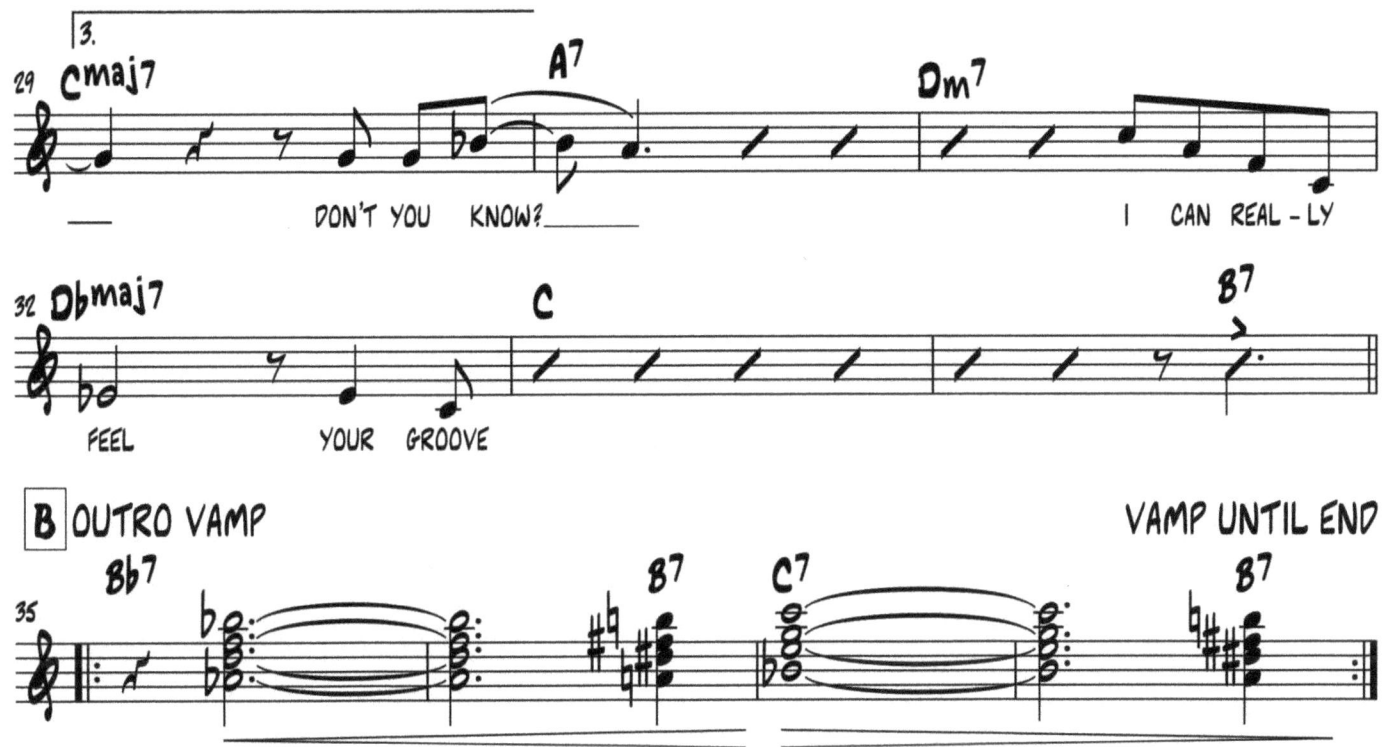

FREE IN AMERICA

BEN SIDRAN

THE NICEST THING ABOUT THE UNITED STATES
EVERYBODY'S FREE TO MAKE THEIR OWN MISTAKES
YOU DON'T HAVE TO LOOK FAR BUT THEN THERE YOU ARE
EVERYONE'S FREE IN AMERICA

YES YOU'RE FREE TO VOTE YOU'RE FREE TO HOPE AGAINST HOPE
YOU'RE FREE TO SPLIT IF YOU DON'T LIKE THE STROKE
MIGHT NOT SOUND LIKE MUCH BUT IT WILL DO IN THE CLUTCH
STEP RIGHT UP SUCKER DON'T BE AFRAID TO TOUCH

'CAUSE YOU'RE FREE (IT'S SO GOOD)
FREE TO MAKE A NEW LIFE (IT'S SO GOOD)
FREE TO CHANGE YOUR NAME
FREE TO CHANGE YOUR GAME
FREE TO CHANGE YOU WIFE
LIFE!

YOU NEVER GIVE IT A SECOND THOUGHT (IT'S SO GOOD)
BUT WHAT YOUR MONEY'S BOUGHT (IT'S SO GOOD)
WELL COAST TO COAST THEY CALL IT THE MOST
SHORE TO SHORE WE GOT LOTS AND LOTS MORE
SEA TO SHINING SEA...FREEDOM
FREEDOM FREEDOM!

ROLL DOWN THE HIGHWAY IN THAT BIG SHINY CAR
GOT THE RADIO TELLING YOU JUST WHERE YOU ARE
MIGHT BE COLD ADVICE BUT THEN YOU CAN'T BEAT THE PRICE
STEP RIGHT UP SUCKER DON'T BE AFRAID OF THE DICE
'CAUSE THE NICEST THING ABOUT THE UNITED STATES
EVERYBODY'S FREE TO MAKE THEIR OWN MISTAKES
YOU DON'T HAVE TO LOOK FAR BUT THEN THERE YOU ARE
IN AMERICA EVERYONE'S FREE

FREE IN AMERICA

I got the idea for the song "Free in America" in the spring of 1975 while lying in a hammock in my backyard, watching the breeze blow pink apple blossoms off the trees. I was thinking about the impending American bicentennial and the blizzard of red, white and blue that would be coming down in a matter of months; by the next summer, it would be a full blown marketing storm and they would be selling patriotic everything before this party was over. The idea of a "Bicentennial Bebop Band" popped into my addled reverie. I could imagine recording a jazz take on the American experience, an alternative to the standard fare that was being planned. I got out of the hammock and went into the house and by evening, I had written the title song. The idea was that no matter how dark things seem in America, one can always leave, which was not the case for folks in many countries around the world. And the thought that "freedom can't be granted, it can only be denied", became a watchword for the lyrics.

FULLNESS OF TIME

BEN SIDRAN

WE'RE HERE BUT FOR A MINUTE
THAT'S ALL THE TIME THAT'S IN IT
WE'RE HERE BUT FOR AN HOUR
LIKE A PASSING SHOWER
WE'RE HERE BUT FOR A DAY
AND THEN WE'RE ON OUR WAY
WE'RE GONE BEFORE WE'RE

HERE BUT FOR A MINUTE
THAT'S ALL THE TIME THAT'S IN IT
WE'RE HERE BUT FOR A WEEK
THERE'S HARDLY TIME TO SPEAK
WE'RE HERE BUT FOR A YEAR
AND NOTHING'S VERY CLEAR
WE'RE GONE BEFORE WE'RE
HERE

IN THE FULLNESS OF TIME
FRUIT FALLS FROM THE VINE
AND THE BRIDGES WE CROSSED
AND THE STAIRS THAT WE CLIMBED
AND THE THINGS THAT WE LOST
THEY'RE ALL FAR BEHIND
IN THE FULLNESS OF TIME

AND SIGHT IS RESTORES
TO THOSE WHO ARE BLIND
AND THE DREAMS OF OUR DAYS
BECOME MEMORIES SUBLIME
IN THE FULLNESS OF TIME
(WE'RE HERE BUT FOR A MINUTE)
IN THE FULLNESS OF TIME
(THAT'S ALL THE TIME THAT'S IN IT)
IN THE FULLNESS OF TIME
(WE'RE HERE BUT FOR AN HOUR)
IN THE FULLNESS OF TIME
(LIKE A PASSING SHOWER)

IN THE FULLNESS OF TIME

GET IT YOURSELF

BEN SIDRAN

SEE THAT ROCK UP ON THE SHELF
YOU WANT THAT ROCK YOU GOT TO GET IT YOURSELF
SEE THAT ROCK UP ON THE SHELF
WELL THERE'S BEEN A LOT OF TALK ABOUT THE FAMILY OF MAN
WELL BROTHER LET ME TELL YOU 'BOUT THE NEW FAMILY PLAN
SEE THAT ROCK YOU GOT TO GET IT
THAT'S RIGHT YOU GOT TO GET IT YOURSELF

SEE THAT ROLL UP ON THE TABLE
YOU WANT THAT ROLE YOU BETTER GET IT WHILE YOU'RE ABLE
SEE THAT ROLL UP ON THE TABLE
WELL LOTS OF FOLKS ARE HUNGRY THAT AIN'T NOTHING NEW
LOT'S OF FOLKS ARE HUNGRIER THAN YOU
SEE THAT ROLL YOU GOT TO GET IT
THAT'S RIGHT YOU GOT TO GET IT YOURSELF
TALKING ABOUT ROCK AND ROLL THAT IS

('CAUSE JIM DANDY TO THE RESCUE) HE AIN'T GONNA COME
(SPACE COWBOY) HE NEVER WAS
(THE GANGSTER OF LOVE AIN'T GONNA SEE ABOUT YOU)
'CAUSE IT'S EVERY MAN FOR HIMSELF
AND EVERY WOMAN TOO

SEE THAT STAR UP IN THE SKY
YOU WANNA BE THAT STAR, YOU BETTER LEARN HOW TO FLY
SEE THAT STAR UP IN THE SKY
GET YOUR ARMS TO FLAPPIN', GET YOUR BEAK INTO THE WIND
LEARN TO FLY WITH THAT MILLION DOLLAR GRIN
SEE THAT STAR, YOU GOT TO GET IT
THAT'S RIGHT, YOU GOT TO GET IT YOURSELF

COPYRIGHT © 1978 BEN SIDRAN
ADMINISTERED BY BULLDOG MUSIC. ALL RIGHTS RESERVED.

GET IT YOURSELF

The rock and roll world is one of fantasy, we all know that, but there was always the hope in the general populace that it would deliver some greater meaning. This song is a kind of admonition to rock and roll fans that if they're looking for something more profound than a music-hall spectacle, they'll have to "get it themselves". Rock on!

GET TO THE POINT

BEN SIDRAN

BABY WON'T YOU GET TO THE
POINT ME TO THE BOTTOM OF
IT'S LOOKING LIKE IT'S NEVER GONNA
STOP ME IF YOU HEARD IT BEFORE
YOU WALK OUT THE DOOR
WHY DON'T YOU DROP IT ON ME
BABY WON'T TO GET THE POINT

THERE'S NOTHING WRONG WITH
LOOKING 'ROUND, I'M LOOK 'ROUND A LITTLE
TOO BAD NOTHING'S HAPPENING HERE FOR
ME AND YOU GOT BETTER THINGS TO
DO YOU WANNA COP A LITTLE
ATTITUDE OR LATITUDE OR
LONGITUDE WILL DO
BUT BABY WON'T YOU GET TO THE POINT

SEE I'VE BEEN WAITING
ANTICIPATING
BUT IT LOOKS LIKE TONIGHT'S A BUST
SO IF YOU MUST KEEP TALKING
IN MY EAR
LET ME MAKE ONE THING
PERFECTLY CLEAR

YOU AND I BEEN BEATING 'ROUND
THE BUSH A LITTLE PUSH
A LITTLE SHOVE A LITTLE LATER
MAYBE WE CAN COP AN
ATTITUDE OR LATITUDE OR
LONGITUDE WILL DO
BUT BABY WON'T YOU GET TO THE
POINT ME TO THE BOTTOM OF
IT'S LOOKING LIKE IT'S NEVER GONNA
STOP ME IF YOU HEARD IT BEFORE
YOU WALK OUT THE DOOR
WHY DON'T YOU DROP IT ON ME
BABY WON'T TO GET THE POINT

GIRL TALK

NEAL HEFTI
LYRICS BY BEN SIDRAN

YOU TAKE YOUR CHANCES WHEN YOU FALL FOR A GIRL LIKE THAT
YOU PAY YOUR MONEY TAKE YOUR CHANCE WITH LOVE AND THAT'S A FACT
THEN LATER ON YOU MAYBE WONDER WHERE SHE'S REALLY AT
BUT LATER ON IT'S LATER ON AND THERE'S NO TURNING BACK
SHE BATS HER EYE YOU WANT TO CRY
SHE SIGHS HER SIGH YOU WANT TO FLY
YOU BETTER RUN DON'T WALK
THAT'S JUST GIRL TALK

SHE'LL TAKE YOUR HAND SHE'LL TAKE YOUR HEART SHE'LL TAKE THE REST OF IT
SHE'LL TAKE YOU MIND SHE'LL TAKE YOUR SOUL SHE'LL TAKE THE BEST OF IT
THEN LATER ON SHE MAYBE WONDERS WHY SHE WANTED THAT
BUT LATER ON IT'S LATER ON AND THERE'S NO TURNING BACK
SHE BATS HER EYE YOU WANT TO CRY
SHE SIGHS HER SIGH YOU WANT TO FLY
YOU BETTER RUN DON'T WALK
THAT'S JUST GIRL TALK

GIRL TALK

NEAL HEFTI
LYRICS BY BEN SIDRAN

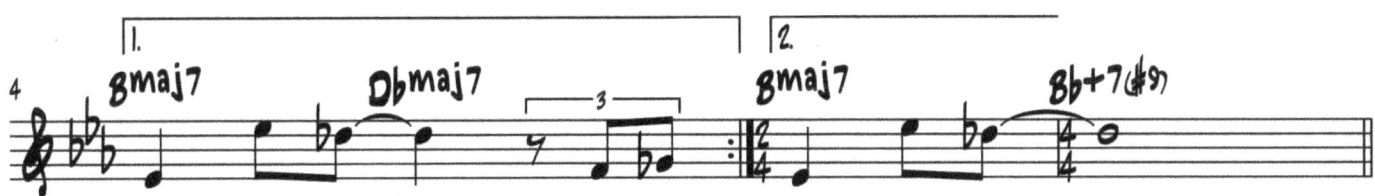
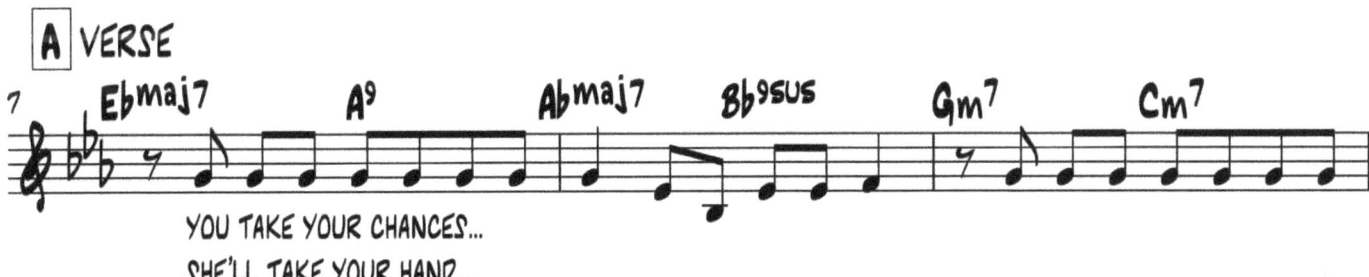

YOU TAKE YOUR CHANCES...
SHE'LL TAKE YOUR HAND...

...RUN DON'T WALK THAT'S JUST GIRL TALK.

COPYRIGHT © 1965 NEAL HEFTI
ADMINISTERED BY SECOND HAND SONGS. ALL RIGHTS RESERVED.

GIRL TALK

Recorded for "The Cat And The Hat", a project where I wrote original lyrics to mostly instrumental jazz standards, this song led me directly into the den of a show business lion. Like many jazz fans, I had long adored the melody of Neil Hefti's "Girl Talk," but found Bobby Troup's original lyrics so outrageously sexist that there was no way to sing them. I had written some new lyrics, replacing the old lines about how women just chatter away over "inconsequential things" with lyrics about the risk of falling in love, but I needed permission from Bobby to record them. I got Bobby on the phone and plunged ahead.

He said, "Yeah, a lot of people want to write new lyrics for that song. I don't see what the problem is with my lyrics."

Instead of going into detail about why the swinger sentiment of the late fifties was no longer apropos, I said, "Bobby, can I just sing you my lyrics now and you can decide for yourself?"

He said, "Sure, kid, take your shot." Over the phone, from two thousand miles away, I sang Bobby Troup my words to "Girl Talk":

When I was done, there was a moment of silence. And then Bobby said, "Okay, I like them. You can record them. But you can never seek the money." I agreed, and to this day, even though several other people have recorded my lyrics to the song, Bobby Troup's estate still collects the royalties.

HAVE YOU HEARD THE NEWS?

BEN SIDRAN

HAVE YOU HEARD THE NEWS
AND DID SHE TELL IT RIGHT
FIRST SHE THREW HIM OUT
AND THEN SHE CALLED HIM BACK IN
HAVE YOU HEARD THE NEWS
AND DID SHE MENTION ME
AT ALL

HAVE I GOT THE BLUES
SITTING HERE TONIGHT
STARING AT THESE WALLS
I WONDER WHO SHE'S BALLING
HAVE I GOT THE BLUES
OR AM I REALLY FREE AT LAST

WOMEN ARE FUNNY
THEY GO ON THAT WAY
TELL YOU THEY'RE YOUR ONLY FRIEND
BUT WHEN YOU WANT AN ANSWER
THE WORDS ARE LIKE CANCER
THEY START TO EAT YOUR HEART OUT

MY SONG'S A LITTLE SAD
DON'T REALLY FEEL THAT BAD
I KNOW THAT THIS WILL PASS
AND THERE'S LOTS OF WAYS OF DYING
BUT HAVE YOU HEARD THE NEWS
AND DID SHE MENTION ME AT ALL

COPYRIGHT © 1972 BEN SIDRAN
ADMINISTERED BY BULLDOG MUSIC. ALL RIGHTS RESERVED.

HAVE YOU HEARD THE NEWS?

I MIGHT BE WRONG

BEN SIDRAN

I MIGHT BE WRONG BUT IT SURE SEEMS TO ME
THE PAST AIN'T WHAT IT WAS
AND THE FUTURE AIN'T WHAT IT USED TO BE
EVERYWHERE I GO I HEAR PEOPLE SAY
MAN, YOU SHOULD HAVE BEEN HERE YESTERDAY

YOU SHOULD HAVE BEEN HERE BEFORE THE FALL
NOW IT'S THE PRICE OF EVERYTHING AND
THE VALUE OF NOTHIN' AT ALL
I MIGHT BE WRONG BUT
I THINK THOSE DAYS ARE GONE
THE PAST AIN'T WHAT IT WAS
AND THE FUTURE WON'T BE HERE LONG.

NOW WE'RE ALL JUST THE SONS OF THE DHARMA BUMS
WADING IN THE WATER OF THE INFINITE FLOW
AND EVERY TIME YOU LOOK
THERE'S ANOTHER DEAD GUY IN YOUR ADDRESS BOOK.
WHERE HAVE ALL THE GOOD ONES GONE?
WHY DID THEY LEAVE US HERE TO CARRY ON?

I MIGHT BE WRONG BUT EVERYWHERE I GO
THEM THAT KNOWS DON'T TALK
AND THEM THAT TALKS DON'T KNOW.
IF SILENCE IS THE ANSWER, WHAT COULD THE QUESTION BE?
I MAY BE WRONG BUT IT SURE SEEMS TO ME
WE WATCH AS TIME PASSES AND THEN SO DO WE

I MIGHT BE WRONG

This song is, in part, a paean to the passing years. We think we know where we're going but we almost always wind up someplace else. And because of that, the past – that period when we were so sure of ourselves and our future – always looks better or, at least, more sure than the present. Particularly when age overtakes our youthful enthusiasm for progress. The line "You should have been here before the fall" refers to the collapse of our hopes and dreams, the "fall" of every great civilization, and also the autumn of our years. "We're all just the sons of the Dharma bums, wading in the water of the infinite flow" references the fact that we are all simply here for a minute and then gone, and that we "watch as time passes and then so do we." I do not find this sad – I find it comforting.

I WANNA BE A BEBOPPER

BEN SIDRAN

I WANNA BE A BEBOPPER
I WANNA GO WHERE THE GOOD ONES GO
I WANNA BE A BEBOPPER
I WANNA KNOW WHAT ALL THE GOOD ONES KNOW
I GOTTA PLAY THOSE SUBSTITUTIONS
LET THE LEADING TONE LIE
I WANNA BE A BEBOPPER UNTIL I DIE

AND I WON'T MIND DYING
IF I CAN HEAR SOMETHING BY BIRD
NOW I WON'T MIND DYING
CAUSE I CAN EASE MY PAIN
IN A MOMENT'S NOTICE WITH COLTRANE
YOU CAN SAY THAT IT'S PASSÉ
BUT THERE'S NO SWEETER WAY TO LET IT PLAY
I GOT TO BE A BEBOPPER
UNTIL I'M THROUGH

NOW THE WHOLE WORLD'S GONE ELECTRIC
THEY'RE ALL PLUGGED INTO THAT ROBOT BAND
YEAH THEY'RE SO ECLECTIC
THERE'S NOTHING THEY WON'T DO
JUST TO DROP THE OTHER SHOE
IT'S MIGHTY HARD TO SEE YOUR HERO
TOSS IT IN FOR A HILL OF BEANS
IT'S HARDER STILL TO CLIMB THAT HILL
WITH A STEINWAY IN YOUR JEANS
BUT RIGHT NOW
I DON'T CARE WHAT THE FREAKS ARE DOING
DOWN THE AVENUE
I GOT TO BE A BEBOPPER UNTIL I'M THROUGH
HOW ABOUT YOU
I GOT TO BE A BEBOPPER UNTIL I'M THROUGH

I WANNA BE A BEBOPPER

73

IN THE BEGINNING

BEN SIDRAN

IN THE BEGINNING MAN CREATED GOD
SO HE WOULD NOT BE ALONE, LOST WITHOUT HOPE
AND GOD BECAME THAT HOPE FOR MAN
AND HOPE BECAME THE REASON TO BELIEVE
THAT GOD CREATED MAN AS PART OF A PLAN
THERE WAS A REASON BEHIND ALL THIS TROUBLE IN MIND

NOW BILLIONS OF PEOPLE BELIEVE WITH THEIR HEARTS
IF THEY HOLD OUT THEIR HAND GOD WILL APPEAR
SO THEY WILL NOT BE ALONE, LOST WITHOUT HOPE
ONLY TO FIND THEY WERE NEVER ALONE
ONLY LOST, LOST IN THE FAMILY OF MAN
AND THAT WAS THE PLAN ALL ALONG.

IN THE BEGINNING

BEN SIDRAN

IN THE BEGINNING

These lyrics started out as a little poem to set the stage for my book *There Was a Fire: Jews, Music and the American Dream*. The book examines the spiritual side of popular music in America and the contribution of the Jewish people to its origins and evolution. I am an atheist; I do not believe there is some overriding sentient force that is tracking me. I also believe that organized religion has been a tremendous cause of human suffering throughout human history – not just through wars and prejudice but through the corruption of everyday language and experience. In wondering how our lives could have been hijacked by such a bizarre idea as an all-seeing, all-knowing entity I came up with this little poem – "In the beginning ... " – and cast it as a traditional blues in the key of G.

IT DIDN'T ALL COME TRUE

BEN SIDRAN

SO IT DIDN'T WORK OUT THE WAY YOU PLANNED
AND YOU'RE NOT THEIR KIND OF LEADING MAN
AND THERE'S NO ONE HERE WHO UNDERSTANDS
THE EMPTINESS YOU FEEL TELL ME WHAT'S FOR REAL
WHERE CAN YOU APPEAL YOUR CASE, A HIGHER COURT
A MOMENT'S GRACE, A LAST RESORT
IS THERE NO ONE HERE TO SEE WHAT YOU CAN SEE
WELL THERE'S ME

I'VE BEEN THERE BEFORE AND I KNOW THE SCORE
AND I'D BE GLAD TO DIRECT YOUR FEET TO THE DOOR
'CAUSE I WANT YOU TO KNOW THAT YOU'RE FREE AND YOU CAN GO

BUT YOU SHOULD KNOW THIS BEFORE YOU DO
YOU'RE GONNA TAKE YOUR TROUBLES THERE WITH YOU
AND THERE'S NOTHING SHE WANTS MORE THAN THAT YOU
BE WHAT YOU CAN BE, SEE WHAT YOU CAN SEE
TAKE A LOOK AT ME BEFORE YOU REALIZE
A SAD MISTAKE A BAD DISGUISE
THERE'S ONLY ONE WAY OUT AND NO SURPRISE

IT'S TRUE
LOOK AT ME AND LOOK AT YOU
WE'RE BOTH FREE TO COMPOSE OUR OWN OPEN AND CLOSE
AND THEN WRITE THE FINAL REVIEW
IT DIDN'T ALL COME TRUE

SO WHEN YOU'RE WAITING FOR THAT MIDNIGHT FLIGHT
AND YOU WANT TO BELIEVE WHAT YOU'RE DOING'S RIGHT
BUT IT GETS SO DARK YOU CANNOT SEE
THE LIGHT BEFORE YOUR EYES THEN YOU REALIZE
IF YOU WANT TO PLAY THE GAME THEN FROM THE START
YOU'RE GONNA LOOSE YOUR BRAIN WHEN YOU BET YOUR HEART
AND THERE'S NO REWARD FOR BEING SMART

IT'S TRUE
LOOK AT ME AND LOOK AT YOU
WE'RE BOTH FREE TO COMPOSE OUR OWN OPEN AND CLOSE
AND THEN WRITE THE FINAL REVIEW
IT DIDN'T ALL COME TRUE

IT DIDN'T ALL COME TRUE

IT DON'T GET NO BETTER

BEN SIDRAN

BILLIONS OF PEOPLE
THOUSANDS OF YEARS
MOUNTAINS OF PAPER
RIVERS OF TEARS
ALL OUR BEST EFFORTS
IS WHAT GOT US HERE
IF WE'RE NOT HAVING FUN
SOMETHING AIN'T CLEAR
CAUSE IT DON'T GET NO BETTER THAN THIS
NO IT DON'T GET NO BETTER THAN THIS

THE BEST AND THE BRIGHTEST
THE WEAK AND THE STRONG
THEY TRIED TO UNITE US
TRIED TO BRING US ALONG
MOUNTAINS OF MUSIC
RIVERS OF SONG SO
IF WE'RE NOT HAVING FUN
THEN WE'RE DOING IT WRONG
CAUSE IT DON'T GET NO BETTER THAN THIS
NO IT DON'T GET NO BETTER THAN THIS

PEOPLE GET READY
NEW SHERIFF IN TOWN
IF ANYONE'S GUILTY
WE'RE ALL GOING DOWN
ONE BAD APPLE
CAN SPOIL THE BUNCH
SO IF YOU CAN'T SHARE THE FOOD
THEN NO ONE GETS LUNCH

IT'S TIME FOR A MEETING
OUT IN DIGITAL SPACE, 'CAUSE
FOR THOUSANDS OF YEARS
WE COULDN'T AGREE ON A PLACE
NOW IT DON'T MATTER
WE JUST SAVING FACE
CAUSE WHEN OUR PARTICLES SCATTER
SPACE IS THE PLACE
AND IT DON'T GET NO BETTER THAN THIS
NO IT DON'T GET NO BETTER THAN THIS

COPYRIGHT © 1988 BEN SIDRAN
ADMINISTERED BY BULLDOG MUSIC. ALL RIGHTS RESERVED.

KING OF HARLEM

(SPOKEN WORD)   BEN SIDRAN

THE RHYTHM OF NEW YORK, NOW THAT'S WHAT HE WAS TALKING ABOUT
THE STREET OF NEW YORK, THE BEAT IN THE STREET OF NEW YORK
LIKE THE HEAT IN NEW YORK IN THE BATHHOUSES, IN THE BACKROOMS
IN THE CHICKEN JOINTS AND THE COTTON CLUBS, BENEATH THE BUILDINGS, BEHIND THE BRIDGES
BENEATH THE SMOKE AND THE MOON, BENEATH THE BENEATH
BUT TUNNELING UP, TUNNELING UP, FROM THE DRY FEET OF NEW YORK
THE BEAT OF NEW YORK, NOW THAT'S WHAT HE WAS TALKING ABOUT
PENA NEGRA, THAT TORTURED THING AT THE HEART OF THE THING
DEEP BENEATH THE THING BUT RISING, RISING

LIKE THE CHARLESTON, CHARLESTON, CHARLESTON
THE BEATING HEART OF NEW YORK, THAT'S WHAT HE WAS TALKING ABOUT
THE NEW YORK CHARLESTON, THAT WOUNDED PULSE AT THE HEART OF NEW YORK
THAT'S WHAT HE WAS TALKING ABOUT, THROBBING, THROBBING BENEATH THE HOWLING MOON
WHERE THE KING OF HARLEM LIKED TO PLAY IT ON A WOODEN SPOON
UP FROM THE STREETS, UP FROM THE FEETS
WHERE THAT GREAT ARSENIC LOBSTER FINALLY LEARNED HOW TO FLY
AND NOW THE MOON IS JUST A SLICE OF RADIANCE DIVINE UP IN THE SKY.
THAT'S WHAT HE WAS TALKING ABOUT. THAT'S WHAT HE WAS TALKING ABOUT.

GO TELL DALI, GO TELL BUNUEL, GO TELL THE MILLIONAIRES IT'S TIME TO SELL
THE FINAL FOOT IS ON THE STAIRS, IT'S TIME TO DRINK THE SILVER WHISKY
THROW THE GLASS INTO THE BRINE 'CAUSE IT'S TIME,

IT'S TIME, IT'S TIME, IT'S TIME IN NEW YORK. YOU GOT NO TIME? BABY YOU GOT NOTHING BUT TIME.
YOU'RE HUSHED BY TIME, CRUSHED BY TIME, NOW THAT'S WHAT HE WAS TALKING ABOUT
PENA NEGRA, THAT TORTURED THING AT THE HEART OF THE THING
DEEP BENEATH THE THING BUT RISING, RISING
FROM BATHHOUSES AND BACKROOMS, LIKE REFUGEES THEY ARRIVED ON BROKEN SHIPS
AND DEPARTED WITH LITTLE MORE THAN THEIR WITS
AY! DIOS MIO! A BROKEN MOON. AND THE WORD WAS RISING, RISING
THAT'S WHAT HE WAS TALKING ABOUT. NOW THAT'S WHAT HE WAS TALKING ABOUT.

GO TELL DALI, GO TELL BUNUEL, GO TELL THE MILLIONAIRES IT'S TIME TO SELL.
THE FINAL FOOT IT'S ON THE STAIRS, THE SPIRE OF SMOKE IS IN THE AIR.

EL MASCARON! EL MASCARON! MIRAD EL MASCARON.
FROM AFRICA TO THE BACKROOMS AND BACKSTAIRS OF COTTON CLUBS AND CHICKEN JOINTS
IN THE MOMENT OF DRY THINGS AND DEAD THINGS
THE BEAT OF NEW YORK. NO RETREAT IN NEW YORK FROM THE HEAT IN NEW YORK.
RELENTLESS. RELENTLESSLY. WITHOUT MERCY. ACROSS WIRED BRIDGES. ABOVE SKY SCRAPERS.
UN MILAGRO! ASSESINADO POR EL CIELO.
A BROKEN MOON HOWLING! HOWLING!
EL MASCARON, EL MASCARON
A WOUNDED PULSE. A BROKEN TUNE.
NOW THAT'S WHAT HE WAS TALKING ABOUT

KING OF HARLEM

In 1998, I was visiting my son Leo in Seville, Spain and we took a little trip to Granada to be with my good friend Georgie Fame. The night before the gig there was a party in the hotel suite of the editor of the El Pais newspaper and it was there that I met Laura Garcia Lorca, the niece of the famed Spanish poet, Federico Garcia Lorca. Laura was the director of the Lorca foundation, dedicated to preserving her uncle's legacy, and several weeks later she invited me to perform at the centenary of his birthday. I became immersed in his writings and translated several of them to my own musical idiom. When Laura came to New York several years later, there was yet another musical performance in his honor and I needed to present a new, additional piece. I was looking through my Lorca collection, reading the "Poet in New York", a long, partly surreal image of his visit to America in 1929, just before the great economic crash. I asked Laura about some of the images he used and she said, "Sometimes a great arsenic lobster is just a great arsenic lobster." These lyrics are my attempt to recall a man wandering a new land at a time of terrible modernism.

LET'S MAKE A DEAL

BEN SIDRAN

WELL YOU GOTTA TAKE A LOOK AT THE AMERICAN DREAM
IT REALLY ISN'T FUNNY
THEY GOT A WAY TO MAKE MONEY
TALK SO LOUD IT'S A SHAME
HAVEN'T GOT IT TELL ME WHO IS TO BLAME
WAITING ON THE MONEY
HEY MAN LET'S MAKE A DEAL

WELL YOU GOTTA TAKE A LISTEN TO AMERICA'S DREAM
SOLID GOLD MONEY
THEY GOT A NON-STOP HONEY
MOON FOR SOMEONE LIKE YOU
YOU KNOW THEY CALL IT TOP FORTY BUT
THEY DON'T REALLY WANT TO
HEY MAN LET'S MAKE A DEAL

WELL YOU GOTTA TAKE A LOOK AT THE AMERICAN DREAM
BEFORE THEY MAKE THE MOVIE
THEY GOT A WAY TO MAKE
LENNY BRUCE COME BACK FOR A BOW
WELL THEY DIDN'T DIG HIM
ANY OLD HOW
THEY'RE JUST WAITING ON THE MOVIE
HEY MAN HERE'S HOW I FEEL
YOU AND ME
LET'S MAKE A DEAL

LIFE'S A LESSON

FRANK ROSOLINO
LYRICS BY BEN SIDRAN

LIFE'S A LESSON, YOU CAN FAIL IT
YOU CAN SET YOUR SPIRIT FREE OR JAIL IT
BUT SETTING IT FREE IS NO GUARANTEE
IT'S GONNA FLY WHEN YOU SAIL IT
THE OBJECT IS TO RIDE IT
BUT SETTING IT FREE WHILE YOU'RE SITTING ASTRIDE IT
ISN'T EASY

YOU CAN LEARN A LOT BY GOING CRAZY
YOU CAN FAIL IT
YOU CAN SET YOUR SPIRIT FREE OR JAIL IT
BUT SETTING IT FREE IS NO GUARANTEE
IT'S GONNA FLY WHEN YOU SAIL IT

AND IF YOU FEEL LIKE YOU'RE IN PRISON
AND NO ONE IS COMING TO TALK OR TO LISTEN
TAKE IT EASY
KNOW THAT NO ONE EVER HAS IT EASY
NO ONE EVER LEARNS TO FLY BY FREEZING
LIFE'S A LESSON YOU CAN PASS OR FAIL

LIFE'S A LESSON

The following is from my memoir, *A Life in the Music*. It recalls the time, in 1979, I was working on the record that became *The Cat And the Hat*. I was writing lyrics for instrumental jazz songs composed by other musicians.

"The (lyrics to the) song that proved the most difficult (to write) was Frank Rosolino's 'Blue Daniel.' Frank was a legend in Los Angeles, a wild, happy-go-lucky guy who sat in the trombone section of Johnny Carson's "Tonight Show" band for years. They called him the 'Silver Fox' because of his rich, white mane and his dapper appearance. He loved to sail and play golf, and he enjoyed a lot of friends, a lovely wife and beautiful kids. All in all, he was on top of the world, leading the ideal jazz life. He had written 'Blue Daniel' in the fifties, and I first heard it on a Cannonball Adderley recording. It was a simple, wistful melody, and when I met Frank back in 1973 I told him I would like to write lyrics for it and wondered if the title meant anything in particular. He said, 'It's just a waltz. Like the Blue Danube. But feel free.'

I made several attempts but always came up short; they seemed too inconsequential for the underlying elegance of Frank's simple little theme. Then one night in 1979 I got a phone call from a friend in L.A. Had I heard about Frank? No, I said, what about Frank? Apparently, he had come home earlier that same day with a gun and, without explanation, shot his family and then himself. There was a long silence. I couldn't say anything. My mind was blank. I was sitting at the piano, so after I hung up, I started playing 'Blue Daniel'. And as if from out of thin air, these lyrics arrived in my head. It was as close as I've ever come to receiving dictation from a higher authority."

LIP SERVICE

BEN SIDRAN

PACIFIC HIGHWAY 1 IT'S A SLOW MOTION DRIVE
TAKE A TOUGH MAN TEN YEARS A PRETTY WOMAN FIVE
IT AIN'T NO DESTINATION JUST A PLACE WHERE YOU ARRIVE
COAST TO COAST THEY CALL IT THE MOST THEY JUST LOVE THAT LEFT COAST JIVE
YOU GET 'EM ON THE PHONE IT'S A DONE DEAL
LOOK 'EM IN THE EYE, OUCH!

LIP SERVICE
MAKES ME NERVOUS
LIP SERVICE
LIKE A BAD ROMANCE
MAKES ME NERVOUS
LIP LIP SERVICE

YOUR BIG CADILLAC IT AIN'T NOTHING BUT A RIDE
YOUR BIG HOUSE ON THE HILL JUST ANOTHER PLACE TO HIDE
YOUR HUNDRED DOLLAR BILL DON'T EVEN COVER LUNCH
YOU CALL A HEART ATTACK A THRILL YOU CALL A SURE THING A HUNCH
YOU GET 'EM ON THE PHONE IT'S A DONE DEAL
LOOK 'EM IN THE EYE, OUCH!

LIP SERVICE
MAKES ME NERVOUS
LIP SERVICE
LIKE A BAD ROMANCE
MAKES ME NERVOUS
LIP LIP SERVICE

LIP SERVICE

BEN SIDRAN

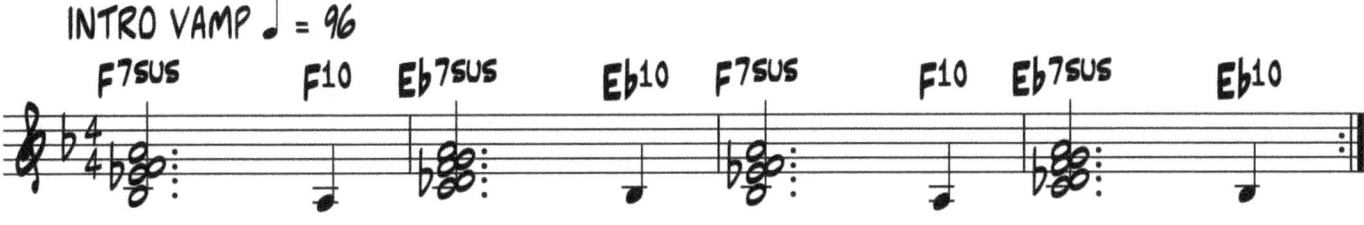

PACIFIC HIGHWAY 1...
YOUR BIG CADILLAC...

...GET 'EM ON THE PHONE...

OUCH! LIP SER-VICE...

MAKES ME NER-VOUS LIP LIP SER-VICE.

COPYRIGHT © 1990 BEN SIDRAN
ADMINISTERED BY BULLDOG MUSIC. ALL RIGHTS RESERVED.

LITTLE SHERRY

CHARLIE ROUSE
LYRICS BY BEN SIDRAN

I WANNA GO AND BE A MOVIE STAR
I WANNA RIDE IN A BIG CARE
LOOKING LIKE A MILLION
I WANNA GO AND GET TO HOLLYWOOD
GO WHILE THE GOING IS STILL GOD
BUT NOTHING THERE CAN TAKE THE PLACE OF YOU
I GOT TO TELL YOU
YOU REALLY GOT ME SKIPPIN'

I GOT THE OFFER JUST THE OTHER DAY
IT CAME FROM QUINCY IN L.A.
HE'S LOOKING FOR A PLAYER
GOT IN THE CAR AND WENT TO YOUR FRONT DOOR
THERE'S SOMETHING FOR ME I KNOW IT
NO ONE NO WHERE CAN TAKE THE PLACE OF YOU
I GOT TO TELL YOU
YOU REALLY GOT ME SKIPPIN'

THERE'S SOMETHING FINE ABOUT YOUR WHOLE DESIGN
THERE'S SOMETHING REAL IN YOUR APPEAL
THEY DON'T HAVE THAT IN L.A.
THERE'S SOMETHING GOOD ABOUT YOUR NEIGHBORHOOD
I THINK IT'S YOU AND YOU KNOW IT
NO ONE NO WHERE CAN TAKE THE PLACE OF YOU
NO ONE CAN DO THE THINGS THAT YOU CAN DO
MY LITTLE SHERRY I'M IN LOVE WITH YOU
I GOT TO TELL YOU
YOU REALLY GOT ME SKIPPIN'

ARRANGEMENT COPYRIGHT © 1983 BEN SIDRAN
ADMINISTERED BY SECOND STORY MUSIC. ALL RIGHTS RESERVED.

LITTLE SHERRY

CHARLIE ROUSE
LYRICS BY BEN SIDRAN

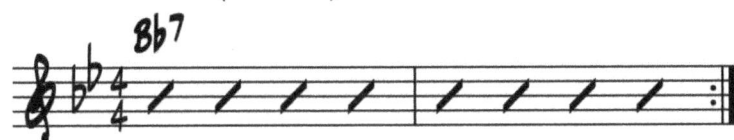

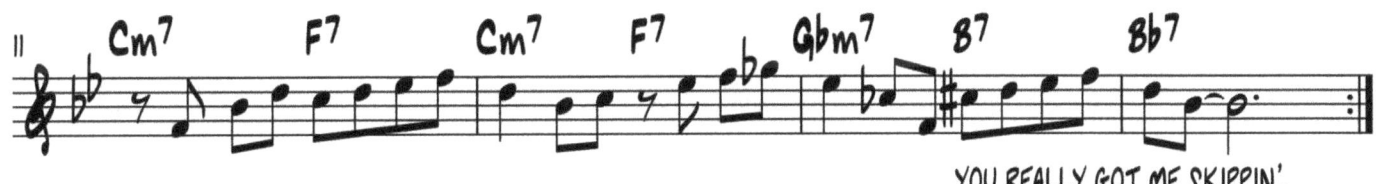
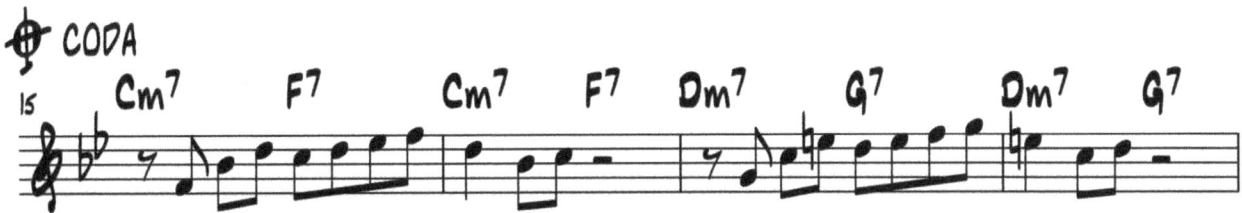

LITTLE SHERRY

I was in Los Angeles often during the 70s and 80s. It's where the music business and the musicians hang was happening. On one trip there, I was visiting my friend Michael Cuscuna who had camped out at Capitol studios to go through all the out-takes from the Blue Note catalog. The Japanese were interested in the label even at a time when American audiences seemed to be indifferent to this amazing cache of music history, and Michael was working with the Japanese to sort out just what was there. There were stacks and stacks of tapes. I was just passing time and picked up a small reel that said "Charlie Rouse" on it, threaded it onto a machine and heard the song "Little Sherry" through the speakers. A great song that had never been released. I eventually called Charlie and told him I would like to write some lyrics to his song and asked what "little Sherry" referred to. He said it was the name of his granddaughter. So I made up this little story about a musician who had the opportunity, the big break really, to go to Hollywood but he didn't want to go because he would miss his "little Sherry".

MIDNIGHT TANGO

BEN SIDRAN

YOU HAVE A CUP OF COFFEE AND ANOTHER CIGARETTE
YOU'RE WAITING FOR YOUR BABY BUT SHE HASN'T SHOWN YET
AND IF SHE DOESN'T MAKE IT WELL YOU'VE GOT NO REGRETS
BECAUSE YOU CAN'T WIN OR LOSE IF YOU AIN'T MADE NO BETS
AND THEN SHE COMES IN WALKING LOOKING FINE AS YOU PLEASE
YOU WANT TO STOP AND DROP RIGHT DOWN ON YOUR KNEES
AND SAY "BABY...YOU DRIVE ME CRAZY"

YOU SAY YOU NEVER WORRY 'CAUSE YOU DON'T NEED A HOME
DON'T NEED AN ADDRESS, DON'T NEED A PHONE
AND YOU DON'T HAVE TO WORRY ABOUT BEING ALONE
'CAUSE YOU CAN MAKE YOUR MUSIC ON A TEN CENT COMB
AND THEN SHE COMES IN WALKING LOOKING FINE AS YOU PLEASE
YOU WANT TO STOP AND DROP RIGHT DOWN ON YOUR KNEES
AND SAY "BABY...YOU DRIVE ME CRAZY"

COPYRIGHT © 1970 BEN SIDRAN
ADMINISTERED BY BULLDOG MUSIC. ALL RIGHTS RESERVED.

MIDNIGHT TANGO

BEN SIDRAN

HAVE A CUP OF COFFEE...
SAY YOU NEVER WORRY...

BA - BY   YOU DRIVE ME CRA - ZY.___ OH.

MIDNIGHT TANGO

In 1969 I realized I could write my own songs. I was late to the party. Bob Dylan changed all the rules. If you weren't writing songs you weren't participating in the discussion. The people I was recording with (Steve Miller and Boz Scaggs) had been doing it for a couple of years and wile I wrote with Steve, and had tried writing poetry when I was in high school I never tried to sit down and put a song together. My first shot was "Midnight Tango" about a young man who was waiting for his girl-friend, thinking he wasn't really invested in whether she came or not, until she finally arrived and in a flash, he realized he was totally taken and she was driving him crazy. The song is set over a series of related minor chords and the melody hovers on one note – a kind of a hypnotic, trancelike feeling, not unlike the feeling of waiting - until she walks in and both the melody and harmony release in relief. When it was done, both Steve and Boz asked to record it, a reward in itself.

MINORITY

GIGI GRYCE
LYRICS BY BEN SIDRAN

THESE ARE SOME HARD TIMES
LOOKING AT THE GOOD SIDE OF CHEAP WINE
GONNA BE SOME SLOW TIMES
WHEN EVERYBODY'S SELLING
AND NOBODY'S BUYING
RICH FOLKS SIMPLY SIGN
THEN THEY TREAT US LIKE WE'RE BLIND
THINK WE CAN'T SEE
WE ARE THE MINORITY
WE'RE JUST TRYING TO GET OFF

LOOKING FOR SOME ACTION
LOOKING FOR SOME REAL LIFE
INSTEAD OF THIS
TRACTION
GOT TO GET THE LAST DROP
FROM EVERY KISS
COME ON BABY
CAN'T RESIST
AIN'T GOT NOTHING
GOT NOTHING TO MISS
YOU AND ME
WE ARE THE MINORITY
WE'RE JUST TRYING TO GET OFF

MINORITY

GIGI GRYCE
LYRICS BY BEN SIDRAN

INTRO & VAMP, SWING ♩ = 188

THESE ARE SOME HARD TIMES...
LOOKING FOR SOME ACTION...

...MINORITY. WE'RE JUST TRYING TO GET OFF.

COPYRIGHT © 1956 GIGI GRYCE
ADMINISTERED BY JACOGG PUBLICATIONS. ALL RIGHTS RESERVED.

MITSUBISHI BOY

BEN SIDRAN

(MELODICALLY SPOKEN WORD)

THEY GROW UP OUTSIDE OF NAGOYA
WHERE THE HOUSES ARE OLD
AND THE GRAVES ARE CAREFULLY TENDED
AND IN THE ANCIENT FIELDS
THEY GROW POWER LINES AND NEON SIGNS
AND THE WORD MITSUBISHI FLOATS LIKE FREEDOM
AND THE SMOKE RISES FROM THE FIRES
WHERE THEY BURN THEIR DESIRES
THEY SAY ANYTHING
NOT TO BE A FAILURE
MITSUBISHI BOY
MITSUBISHI BOY

THEY GROW UP OUTSIDE OF SAPPORO
WHERE THE HOUSES ARE NEW
AND THE GRAVES ARE CAREFULLY TENDED
WEAR THE MASK, PUMP THE GAS, STAND IN LINE, DRINK THE WINE
HANG UP THE WASHING IN THE RAIN TO DRY OUT ON THE LINE
AND THE SMOKE RISES FROM THE FIRES
WHERE THEY BURN THEIR DESIRES
THEY SAY ANYTHING
NOT TO BE A FAILURE
MITSUBISHI BOY
MITSUBISHI BOY

THE HAIKU OF FAST FOOD
THE RAIN AND THE SMOKE
THE SKY IS CRYING
NOBODY GETS THE JOKE
THE TRAIN MOVES TOO FAST TO MAKE OUT THE FACE IN THE WINDOW
THE TRAIN MOVES SO FAST IT HAS ONE LONG WINDOW FACELESS
AND THE SMOKE RISES FROM THE FIRES
WHERE THEY BURN THEIR DESIRES
THEY SAY ANYTHING
NOT TO BE A FAILURE
MITSUBISHI BOY
MITSUBISHI BOY

COPYRIGHT © 1982 BEN SIDRAN
ADMINISTERED BY BULLDOG MUSIC. ALL RIGHTS RESERVED.

MITSUBISHI BOY

In 1985, I was in Japan. One day, while riding on the bullet train from Tokyo to Osaka with my friend Nobu Yoshinari, I asked him to tell me something I might not know about the Japanese culture. He said, "Do you know about the Mitsubishi Boy?"

I said, "No, what is a Mitsubishi Boy?" "It's like a company man, only more intense." "What would a Mitsubishi Boy say?" "Anything, just not to be a failure."

Out the window of the speeding train, I saw fires in the fields, laundry hung out in the rain, miles and miles of housing. I started writing the song "Mitsubishi Boy" then and there, literally chronicling what I was seeing out the window.

THE SONGS OF BEN SIDRAN 1970-2020, Vol. 1

MONK'S MOOD

**THELONIOUS MONK
LYRICS BY BEN SIDRAN**

YOU AND I TOGETHER
EVER A BRAVE NEW START
AS WE GROW OLD DEAR
SONGS THAT WE HOLD DEAR
PLAY FOR THE DAY
WE PART

YOU AND I FOREVER
NEVER NO MORE TO PART
TIME DOESN'T PASS,
IT'S WINE IN OUR GLASS
LET'S DRINK NOW
TO DRYING'S LAST ART

AND WHEN WE'RE GONE
WHO WILL CARRY ON
WHO WILL REMEMBER TODAY
THOSE WHO ARE STRONG
WILL CARRY US ON
AND MUSIC WILL SHOW THEM
THE WAY

YOU AND I COMPLETELY
SO SWEETLY WE PLAY
OUR PART
TURNING THE PAGE
CROSSING THE STAGE
WE BOW ONCE TO LIFE
AND WE DEPART

MONK'S MOOD

Thelonious Monk's romance with his wife Nellie is legendary. She cared for him through thick and thin, always making sure he had what he needed to make his music. I was thinking about this great love when I wrote these lyrics. One day, several years later, after the recording of the song was made, Mose Allison told me "This is your contribution."

Recording Bop City with Peter Erskine, Eddie Gomez, Mike Mainieri and Phil Woods. 1982.

NARDIS

MILES DAVIS
LYRICS BY BEN SIDRAN

SOMEWHERE
OUT ON THE RUSSIAN PLAIN
ONE MAN ONE NIGHT
CAUGHT ONE FAST TRAIN

ALONE
HE TRAVELED NIGHT AND DAY
NOT KNOW WHERE
HIS FUTURE LAY

IN TIME
HE BECAME RESIGNED
USING HIS HANDS
BUT NOT HIS MIND

AND NOW
HIS MEMORY'S ALL BUT LOST
THERE'S JUST THIS SONG
AT SUCH A COST

NARDIS

I asked Miles Davis, who wrote the music, why he named it "Nardis". He thought for a minute and said, 'I don't know. I wrote it for Cannonball (Adderley). Why? What does it mean?" I said, "I don't know but it's my last name backwards. He said, "I didn't know that. Nice name!"

The lyrics I wrote for it speak about my father who was born in Eastern Europe, in the Pale of Settlement, and came to America as a young boy. It's not the literal truth of his personal story, more of a metaphor for how his life played out.

OLD HOAGY

BEN SIDRAN

SING ME A LOVE SONG, OLD FASHIONED LOVE SONG
TAKE ME RIGHT ON BACK
TO THE PLACE WHERE WE STARTED YOUNG AND BROKEN HEARTED

JUST TWO KIDS DREAMING, LAUGHING AND SCHEMING
OUR LOVE WAS MAGIC THEN, OUR LOVE WAS TRAGIC THEN

KIND OF LIKE A MOVIE, OLD HOLLYWOOD MOVIE
YOU KNOW, WHERE THE BAND IS BREAKING UP
WE'LL BE THE COUPLE THAT'S MAKING UP
WELL IT'S GONE BUT THE MEMORY
SEEMS TO LINGER THROUGH THE MOONLIGHT
DRIFTING THROUGH THE GEORGIA PINES
AND OVER IN THE CORNER

THERE'S OLD HOAGY JUST SINGING ABOUT OUR LOVE
CIGARETTE HANGING OUT OF THE CORNER OF HIS MOUTH
THERE'S OLD HOAGY JUST SINGING ABOUT OUR LOVE

TELL ME A STORY OF THE DAYS GONE TO GLORY
ONE WHERE THE GOOD GUY GETS THE GIRL, THAT'S MY KIND OF WORLD

SING ME THAT LOVE SONG, THAT OLD FASHIONED LOVE SONG
OUR LOVE WAS MAGIC THEN, OUR LOVE WAS TRAGIC THEN

KIND OF LIKE A MOVIE, OLD BLACK AND WHITE MOVIE
WHERE THE BAND IS BREAKING UP, PASSING OUT SMOKES, TELLING OLD JOKES

THEN THEY'RE GONE BUT THE MEMORY SEEMS TO LINGER LIKE THE MOONLIGHT
DRIFTING THROUGH THE GEORGIA PINES
AND OVER IN THE CORNER

THERE'S OLD HOAGY JUST SINGING ABOUT OUR LOVE
CIGARETTE HANGING OUT OF THE CORNER OF HIS MOUTH
THERE'S OLD HOAGY JUST SINGING ABOUT OUR LOVE

HE'S SINGING "GEORIA, GEORGIA ON MY MIND...."
THERE'S OLD HOAGY JUST SINGING ABOUT OUR LOVE

OLD HOAGY

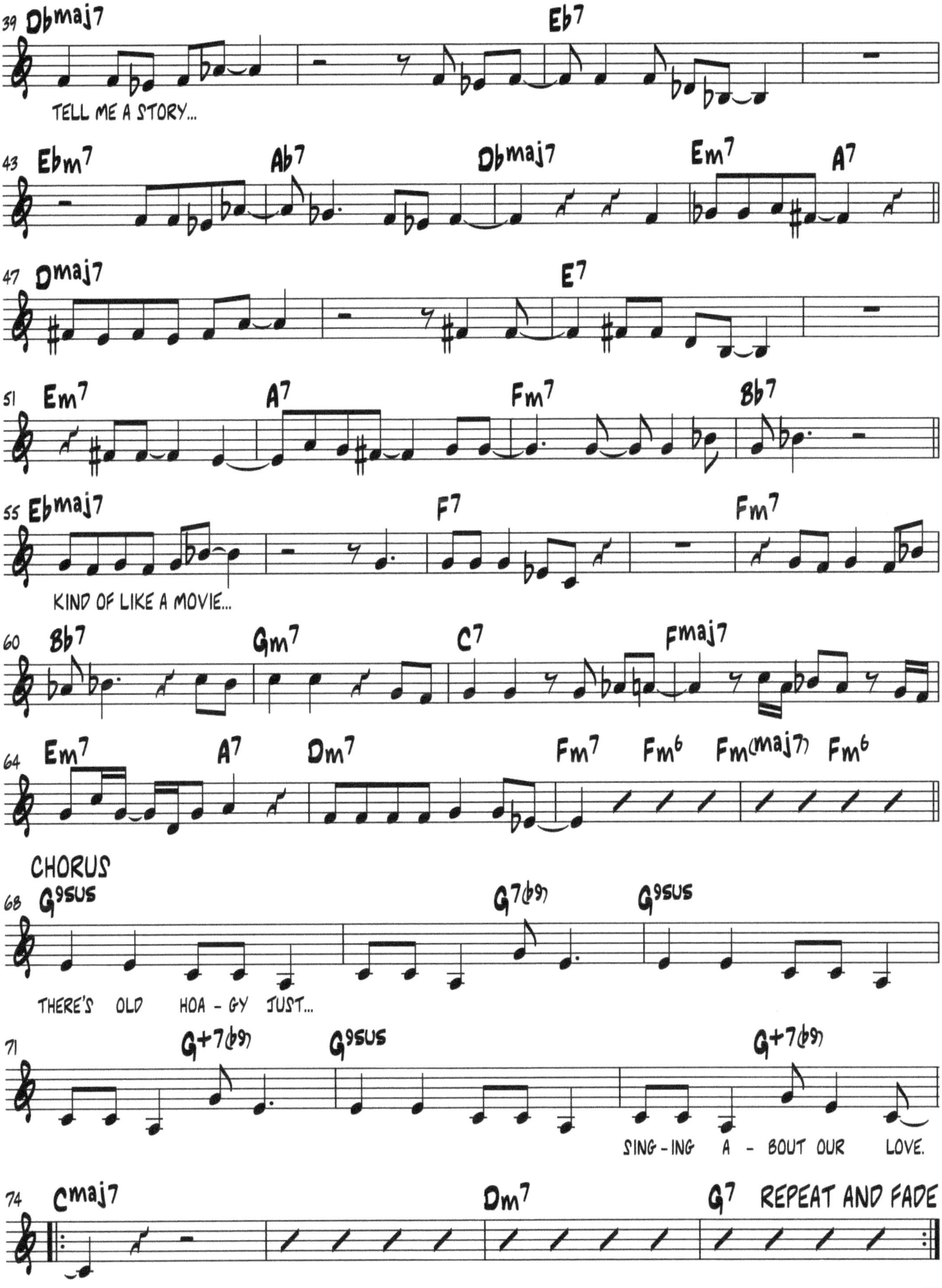
39 Dbmaj7
Eb7
TELL ME A STORY...
43 Ebm7
Ab7
Dbmaj7
Em7
A7
47 Dmaj7
E7
51 Em7
A7
Fm7
Bb7
55 Ebmaj7
F7
Fm7
KIND OF LIKE A MOVIE...
60 Bb7
Gm7
C7
Fmaj7
64 Em7
A7
Dm7
Fm7
Fm6
Fm(maj7)
Fm6
CHORUS
68 G9sus
G7(b9)
G9sus
THERE'S OLD HOA - GY JUST...
71
G+7(b9)
G9sus
G+7(b9)
SING - ING A - BOUT OUR LOVE.
74 Cmaj7
Dm7
G7
REPEAT AND FADE

Recording Old Songs For The New Depression
with Buddy Williams, Marcus Miller and Richie Cole. 1981.

ON THE COOL SIDE

BEN SIDRAN

(SPOKEN WORD)

YOU KNOW, SOMETIMES IT SEEMS LIKE ALL THE GOOD TIMES ARE GONE
BUT GOT TO KEEP ON PUSHING, YOU GOT TO KEEP ON KEEPIN' ON (KEEP ON KEEPIN' ON)
FOR EXAMPLE, TAKE ME SITTING UP HERE TODAY
I WOULDN'T BE WITH YOU IF I BELIEVED THE THINGS THAT THE PEOPLE SAY

YOU GOT TO KEEP ON SEARCHING (KEEP ON SEARCHING)
KEEP IT ON THE COOL SIDE (KEEP IT ON THE COOL SIDE)
KEEP ON KEEPING ON

THEY SAY YOU WON'T FIND WATER DIGGING IN THE SAND
BUT YOU KEEP RIGHT ON DIGGING
YOU MIGHT FIND YOUR OWN LEMONADE STAND (TROPICANA POOL SIDE)
THEY SAY YOU WON'T FIND YOUR DINNER
LOOKING UP IN THE SKY
BUT YOU KEEP YOUR EYES WIDE OPEN
ALL FOUR COURSES MIGHT FLY BY
YOU GOT TO KEEP ON SEARCHING (KEEP ON SEARCHING)

KEEP IT ON THE COOL SIDE (KEEP IT ON THE COOL SIDE)
KEEP ON KEEPING ON
KEEP ON SEARCHING (KEEP ON SEARCHING)
KEEP IT ON THE COOL SIDE (KEEP IT ON THE COOL SIDE)
KEEP ON KEEPING ON

AND WHEN YOU GET A LITTLE TIRED
AND YOU CAN'T FIND A PLACE TO REST
AND WHAT USED TO BE EASY
IS NOW SOME KIND OF TEST
JUST REMEMBER
THERE'S NO SUBSTITUTE FOR LIFE
YOU WOULDN'T EVEN KNOW YOU WERE LIVING
IF IT WEREN'T FOR ALL THIS PAIN AND STRIFE
YOU GOT TO KEEP ON SEARCHING (KEEP ON SEARCHING)

KEEP IT ON THE COOL SIDE (KEEP IT ON THE COOL SIDE)
KEEP ON KEEPING ON
KEEP ON SEARCHING (KEEP ON SEARCHING)
KEEP IT ON THE COOL SIDE (KEEP IT ON THE COOL SIDE) KEEP ON KEEPING ON

PIANO PLAYERS

BEN SIDRAN

THEY PLAYED PIANO AND IT WENT LIKE THIS
THEY COULD SWING AS SWEETLY AS AN ANGEL'S KISS
HEARING GEORGE SHEARING RUNNING STEADY WITH
FREDDY REDD, YES
TALK ABOUT PIANO
PLAYERS IN THE PAST THEY REALLY KNEW HOW TO FLY
A ONE WAY TRIP ON A MAGIC CARPET RIDE
IN THE PARK WITH SONNY CLARK OR WALKING THROUGH THE DARK
WITH BUD POWELL
WON'T YOU LISTEN TO THEM

WALTER BISHOP, WALTER NORRIS
WALTER DAVIS AND WALL TO WALL EXPLORES LIKE
WYNTON KELLY AND OOO ART TATUM
PHINNEAUS, THELONIOUS, ANYWAY YOU RATE EM

THE MUSIC THAT THEY MADE IT'S A LIVE TODAY
CAUSE WHEN YOU HEAR CECIL TAYLOR YOU HEAR JELLY ROLL PLAY
AND NEARING THAT CLEARING YOU'RE HEARING THE REAL MCCOY
ROLL EM ROY

HORACE SILVER HORACE PARLAN
BARRY HARRIS DON'T YOU DARE FORGET RED GARLAND
HERBIE NICHOLS, HAROLD MAYBURN
FLANAGAN, ELLIGTON, JAY MCSHANN

THEY BURN MORE BRIGHTLY RIGHTLY TODAY
BECAUSE NOTHING IN THE WORLD WILL TAKE YOUR BREATH AWAY
LIKE COUNT BASIE FATS WALLER PINE TOP ERROL GARNER
HAMP HAWES NORMAN SIMMONS KENNY DREW BOBBY TIMMONS
DUKE PEARSON DUKE JORDAN HANK JONES STILL RECORDIN
OSCAR GOT THE GRAMMEY, BILL EVANS PUT THE WHAMMY ON MILES
PUT IT ON MILES, PUT IT ON MILES, PUT IT ON MILES....

BENNY GREEN HE'S ON THE SCENE
AND LARRY GOLDINGS' HOLDING SOMETHING MEAN
AND BRAD MALDAU HE GOT THE POWER
BUT DAVE HAZELTINE HE'S GOT MY MIND ALL

MESSED UP YOU GUESSED UP TO NOW
I BEEN BACK IN THE PAST
CAUSE I BELIEVE SOMEHOW
NOTHING SAYS LOVIN' LIKE A GENE HARRIS WALKING BLUES
THAT'S SOME NASTY SHOES

THEY GOT A HALL IN PARIS IT'S A CITY BLOCK LONG
WALL TO WALL PICTURES
JUST PICTURE IT GONE
THAT'S WHAT WE'RE MISSING
EVERY DAY WE DON'T LISTEN TO

CEDAR AND RAMSEY, MICHEL AND AHMAD
KEITH, CHICK AND HERBIE, TALKING BOUT GOD
WILLY PICKENS, YOU FEEL THE PLOT THICKENS
TOMMY FLANAGAN, FEEL LIKE A MAN AGAIN
LES MCCANN GOT THE GREAT LEFT HAND
ELMO HOPE HAD THE REAL GOOD DOPE
NOW SILKEN SOUL, THAT'S NAT KING COLE
TAKING THE CHANCE WITH JUNIOR MANCE
TAKING A PAGE FROM MOSE..AND CLOSE.

COPYRIGHT © 1982 BEN SIDRAN
ADMINISTERED BY BULLDOG MUSIC. ALL RIGHTS RESERVED.

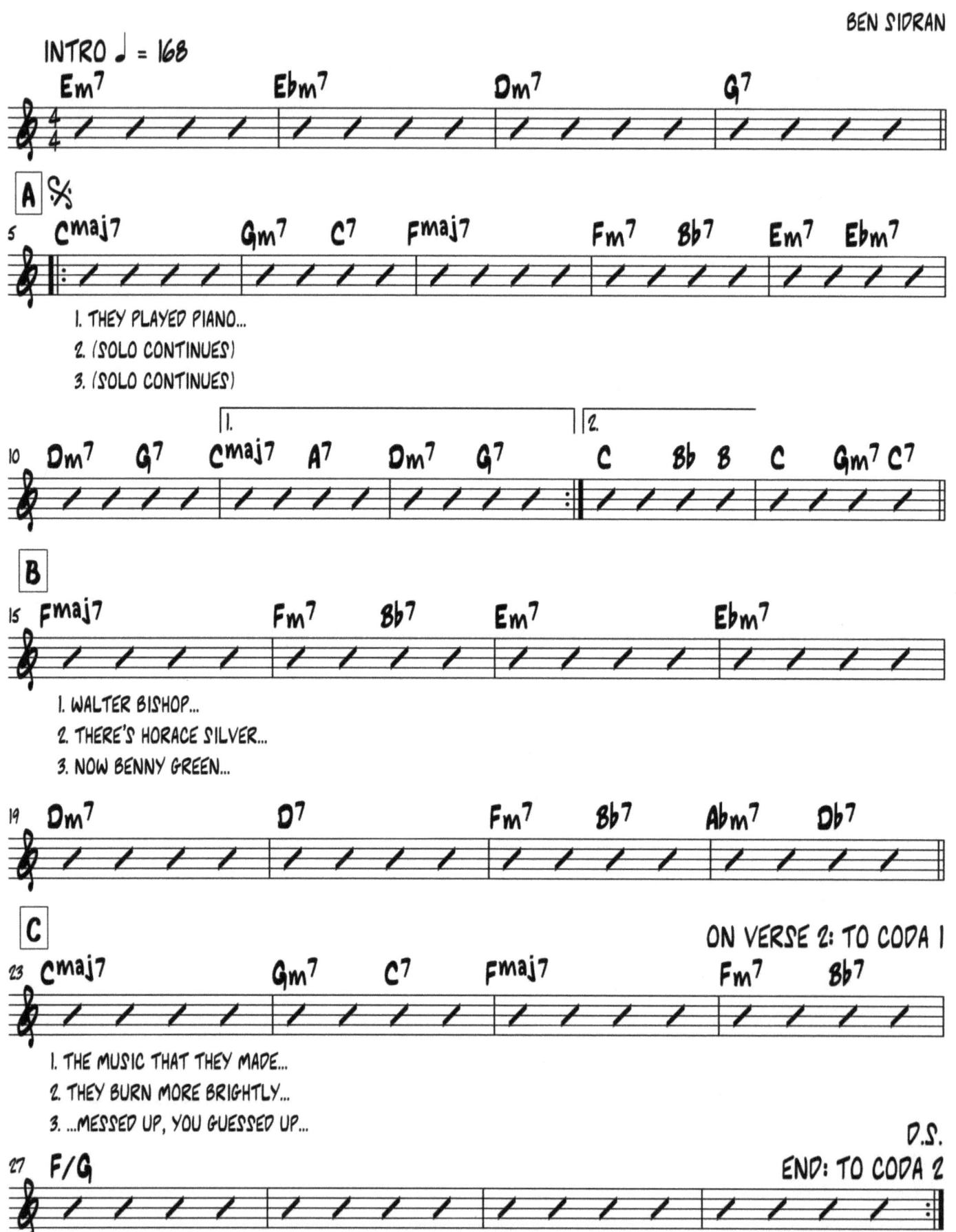

PIANO PLAYERS

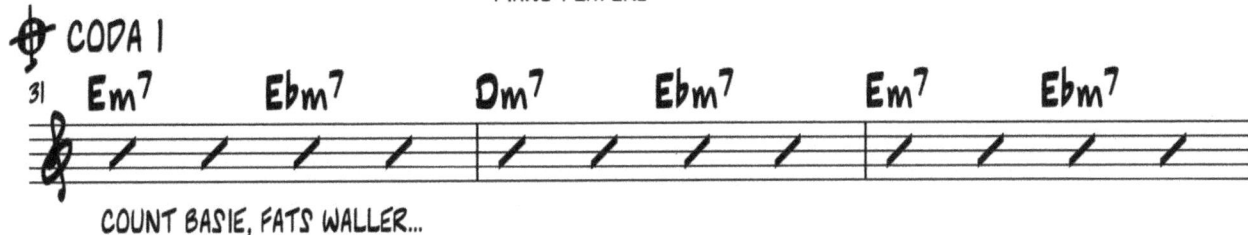

COUNT BASIE, FATS WALLER...

DUKE PEARSON...

...WHAMMY ON MILES... ...PUT IT ON MILES... ...PUT IT ON MILES... TO B AND MORE SOLOS

...TO CEDAR AND RAMSEY...

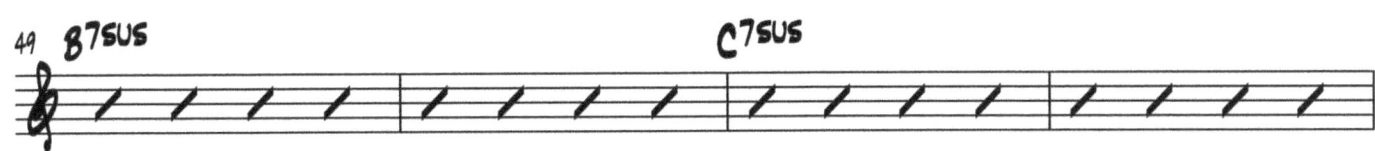

...TAKING THE CHANCE...

PIANO PLAYERS

I wrote this lyric as a kind of throw-away, just calling out some of my favorite piano players. I didn't intend to record it – I didn't think it was a real song or that anyone would be interested in it. Just shows you how little we know about who and where we are. When I was making the record Old Songs For The New Depression, I was just finishing up the sessions and a friend came down to listen to the playbacks. Sitting in the control room, he said, "What ever happened to that song you wrote about all the piano players?" I had sung it to him over the phone months before and had completely forgotten about it. He said, "You should really record that," and so I got Buddy Williams and Marcus Miller, who were packing up their gear, back in the studio and we cut it, just like that. Six months later, when the record was released it made it to number one on the jazz charts (of course, we know what that's worth) and "Piano Players" was "the hit".

Over the years, it has become very popular, particularly among jazz musicians. In fact, one night in a little club in Brussels, I heard a sharp voice over my shoulder say, "Play that piano players song." I turned around to see Michel Petrucciani sitting at a table behind me. The next day, I wrote several more verses and, naturally, included Michel in the list.

PICTURE HIM HAPPY

BEN SIDRAN

(SPOKEN WORD)

THERE'S A MAN AND A ROCK AND A REAL STEEP HILL
SUN IS SO HOT EVEN THE SHADOWS CAN KILL
HE KEEPS RIGHT ON PUSHING TRYIN TO GET TO THE TOP
BUT THE FORCES OF NATURE TRY MAKE A MAN DROP
HE'S DOWN ON HIS KNEES IN A WORLD FULL OF PAIN
BUT TIME AFTER TIME, HE GETS BACK UP AGAIN
YOU GOT THE PICTURE
YOU GOT TO PICTURE HIM HAPPY

THE SUN IS THE TRUTH AND THERE'S NO PLACE TO HIDE
THE ROCK IS TIME PASSING AND TIME WILL ABIDE
THE HILL IS THE SHAPE OF ALL THINGS TO COME
AND THE MAN HE'S JUST SUFFERING IN THE HEAT AND THE SUN
TRYIN' TO FIND SOME MEANING IN A WORLD THAT DON'T CARE
BUT THE ROCK WON'T TALK AND THE HILL DON'T SHARE
YOU GOT THE PICTURE
YOU GOT TO PICTURE HIM HAPPY
PICTURE HIM HAPPY

NOW IT AINT WHAT YOU DO IT'S THE WAY THAT YOU DO IT
IT AINT WHERE YOU GO ITS THE WAY THAT YOU GO THROUGH IT
DESPERATE TIMES CALL FOR DESPERATE ACTIONS
DESPERATE MINDS DESPERATE DISTRACTIONS

THE SUN IS SO HOT THAT YOU CAN'T BREATH THE AIR
IT'S AN EYE FOR AN EYE AND EVERYTHING IS FAIR
TRY TO FIND A REASON IN A WORLD WHERE THERE'S NONE
THERE'S JUST THIS ROCK AND THIS HILL AND THIS GOD DAMNED SUN
BUT WHEN HE GETS NEAR THE TOP THERE'S A TERRIBLE THRILL
HE SEES ANOTHER MAN AND ANOTHER ROCK GOING UP ANOTHER HILL
YOU GOT THE PICTURE
YOU GOT TO PICTURE HIM HAPPY

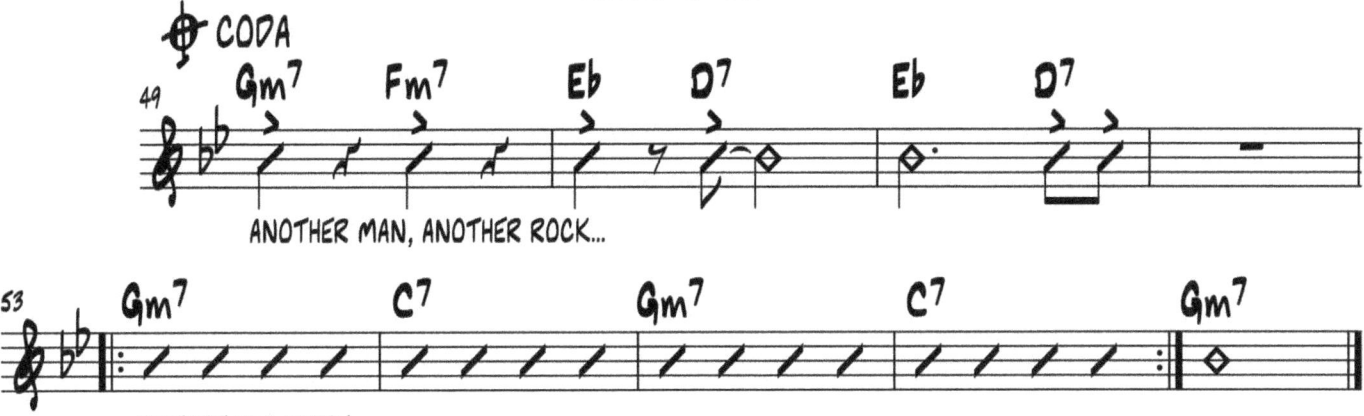

PRIVATE GUY

BEN SIDRAN

WHEN NOBODY'S LOOKING
THATS WHEN I'M COOKIN'
WHEN NOBODY'S WAITING
I'M ELEVATIN'
WHEN NOBODY'S CARIN'
I'M SOUL BARIN'
WHEN NOBODY'S PUSHIN'
AND I GOT ME A CUSHIN'
YEAH I TRIED AND I TRIED
BUT I REALIZED I'M JUST A PRIVATE GUY

WHEN NOBODY'S KNOCKIN'
I'M STEADY ROCKIN'
WHEN NOBODY'S CALLIN'
THAT'S WHEN I'M BALLIN'
WHEN NOBODY'S ASKIN'
I'M MULTI-TASKIN'
BUT WHEN THEY'RE HANDING OUT PRIZES
I'M WEARING DISGUISES
YEAH I TRIED AND I TRIED
BUT I REALIZED I'M JUST A PRIVATE
I TRIED TO HIDE CAUSE
I REALIZED I'M JUST A PRIVATE GUY

WHEN NOBODY'S HOPIN'
THAT'S WHEN I'M COPIN'
WHEN NOBODY'S RIGHT UP
THAT'S WHEN I LIGHT UP
WHEN NOTHING IS JUMPIN'
MY HEART IS PUMPIN'
WHEN NOBODY WANTS ME
THE GROOVE IT JUST HAUNTS ME
YEAH I TRIED AND I TRIED
BUT I REALIZED I'M JUST A PRIVATE
I TRIED TO HIDE CAUSE
I REALIZED I'M JUST A PRIVATE GUY

PRIVATE GUY

A RICH INTERIOR LIFE

BEN SIDRAN

I GOTTA PULL UP MY PANTS
I GOTTA KICK OFF MY SHOES
I GOTTA LEARN HOW TO DANCE
I GOTTA THROWN DOWN THESE BLUES
GOTTA WARM UP THE BREAD
GOTTA PAY OFF THESE DUES
I GOT A RICH INTERIOR LIFE

I GOTTA LIGHTEN MY LOAD
I GOTTA LOOSEN MY TIE
I GOT TO TIGHTEN MY ACT
I GOT TO LEARN HOW TO FLY
CAUSE SOONER OR LATER AND PROBABLY NOT LATER
I GOTTA TURN ON THE LIGHT
OR MAYBE DON'T EVEN TRY
I GOT A RICH INTERIOR LIFE

THERE'S A THING THAT THEY SAY
OR MAYBE SOMETHING I READ
OR A SMELL IN THE AIR
OR A SOUND IN MY HEAD
IF I DON'T WRITE IT DOWN I'M GONNA WISH THAT I DID
TAKE THE BULL BY THE HORNS
AND PUT IT TO BED

I GOTTA PICK UP THE PIECES
I GOTTA STRAIGHTEN THE CREASES
I GOTTA REWRITE THE THESIS
BEFORE IT ALL CEASES
OR MAYBE JUST WAIT AND READ THE PRESS RELEASES
I GOT A RICH INTERIOR LIFE

2019, Seville, Spain. Photo by Amanda Sidran.

SEARCHING FOR A GIRL LIKE YOU

BEN SIDRAN

I'M SEARCHING I'M GOING OUT OF MIND
I'M KIND OF DESPERATE TRYING TO FIND
SOMEONE SPECIAL
SEARCHING FOR A GIRL LIKE YOU

TIME IS PASSING
I FEEL MYSELF GETTING OLD
BUT LIKE A MAN WHO'S DROWNING
I NEED SOMETHING I CAN HOLD
SOMETHING SPECIAL
SEARCHING FOR A GIRL LIKE YOU

AND EVERY DAY WHEN THE SUN IS GOING DOWN
FIND ME SEARCHING IN ANOTHER PART OF TOWN
IT'S GETTING COLD OUT
I GOTTA HOLD OUT
FOLKS SAY I SHOULDN'T CARE
I KNOW YOU'LL BE RIGHT THERE

WHY AM I LIVING
THAT'S WHAT OTHER PEOPLE ASK
BUT I'M A MAN WHO'S DRIVEN
AND BABY YOU'RE MY TASK
YOU'RE SOMETHING SPECIAL
SEARCHING FOR A GIRL LIKE YOU

GONNA FIND YOU TOO

IT'S GONNA HAPPEN
JUST LIKE EVERYTHING THAT'S GOOD
UNEXPECTED
JUST WHEN I THOUGH IT NEVER COULD
YOU'RE SOMETHING SPECIAL
I'M SEARCHING FOR A GIRL LIKE You babe...

SEARCHING FOR A GIRL LIKE YOU

SEE YOU ON THE OTHER SIDE

BEN SIDRAN

(MELODICALLY SPOKEN WORD)

EVERYBODY WANTS TO BE A STAR
DON'T CARE WHERE THEY'RE GOING
BUT THEY WANT TO GO FAR
I CAN'T GO WITH YOU
BUT YOU CAN DRIVE MY CAR
AND I'LL SEE YOU ON THE OTHER SIDE

YOU WANT TO RUN FOR OFFICE
YOU WANT TO CUT A HIT
YOU REALLY WANT TO BE IN PICTURES
AIN'T THAT IT
I CAN'T VOTE FOR YOU
BUT WHEN YOU QUIT
I'LL SEE YOU ON THE OTHER SIDE

SOMETIME IN THE NAME OF JUSTICE
SOMETIME IN THE NAME OF SOUL
ONE TIME HE WANTS TO BUST US
THE NEXT MINUTE HE'S GOT A GOAL IN LIFE
A GOLDEN DREAM
TO HELP US ACROSS LIFE'S STREAM
AND ALL WE GOTTA DO IS

SUPPORT HIS HABIT FOR FAME AND SUCCESS
LET HIM GRAB IT AND HE'LL STRAIGHTEN THIS MESS
WELL HE CAN HAVE IT
I CONFESS
I'LL SEE YOU ON THE OTHER SIDE

SEE YOU ON THE OTHER SIDE

BEN SIDRAN

SHE STEPS INTO A DREAM

BEN SIDRAN

AN ORDINARY DAY IN AN ORDINARY TOWN
NOTHING IS OUT OF PLACE EXCEPT SHE'S LEAVING (SHE'S LEAVING)
HAT IN HAND DOWN AT THE TAXI STAND
SHE WAS RIGHT, SHE WAS WRONG
NOW SHE'S DEFINITELY GONE
(MAGIC)
SHE STEPS INTO A DREAM

A LITTLE LATER ON HE FINALLY FINDS THE NOTE
NOTHING IS OUT OF PLACE EXCEPT SHE'S GONE NOW (SHE'S GONE NOW)
HEAD IN HAND HE DOESN'T UNDERSTAND
WAS HE RIGHT WAS HE WRONG WELL SHE'S DEFINITELY GONE
(MAGIC)

JUST TAKE A LOOK AT ALL THE PEOPLE THAT WERE PASSING
THE CURRENT CARRIES THEM IT CARRIES ON SO STRONG
IT'S HARD TO SEPARATE THE DREAMING FROM THE DREAMER
THIS DREAM HAS CARRIED ON SO LONG
SHE STEPS INTO A DREAM...

THE CREDITS ROLL SHE THINKS SHE GETS THE STORY
NOTHING ABOUT THE PLOT REVEALS THE MEANING OF DREAMING
THE ENDING WASN'T SAD WHY DOES SHE FEEL SO SAD
WAS IT LIES WAS IT TRUTH OR JUST ANOTHER TICKET AT THE BOOTH
SHE STEPS INTO A DREAM...

THE LATE NIGHT SHOW IT'S LAUGHING IN THE CORNER
A FLICKERING LIGHT REVEALS THE HEARTBREAK (THE HEARTBREAK)
HE TOOK IT ON THE CHIN SHE GAVE IT BACK TO HIM
SHE WAS HERE SHE WAS GONE JUST ANOTHER TOP FORTY SONG
SHE STEPS INTO A DREAM...

SO LONG

BEN SIDRAN

RAINDROPS RUN TO RIVERS
RIVERS RUN TO SEA
SEA TURNS INTO THUNDER
BRINGS THOSE RAINDROPS BACK TO ME
LOVE IS LIKE THOSE RAINDROPS
GENTLE AND SO STRONG
IT CAN SAVE ME WHEN I'M THIRSTY
I'VE BEEN THIRSTY OH SO LONG
I'M NOT LOST IF YOU CAN FIND ME
YOU CAN'T FIND ME TILL I'M GONE
I'VE BEEN THIRSTY OH SO LONG

MAN CRIES INTO DARKNESS
DARKNESS HAS NO EARS
BUT THAT'S JUST WHERE THE WIND BEGINS
AND THE WIND WILL BLOW FOR YEARS
IT'S THE WIND THAT CARVES THE CANYON
THE WIND THAT BRINGS THE RAIN
LISTEN TO THE WIND TONIGHT
THE WIND WILL CALL YOUR NAME
1 MAN CRIES INTO DARKNESS
DARKNESS HAS NO EARS
LISTEN TO THE WIND TONIGHT
IT'S COMING ACROSS THE YEARS

THERE'S A MAN WAITING BY THE OCEAN
FOR THE SHIP THAT WON'T COME IN
THE TIDE IS ROLLING STEADY
THE CHANCE IS GETTING THIN
ACROSS THE DARK HORIZON
HE THINKS HE SEES A MAST
BUT THE SHIP JUST KEEPS ON SAILING
AND THE HOPE IS FADING FAST
I'M NOT LOST IF YOU CAN FIND ME
YOU CAN'T FIND ME UNTIL I'M GONE
A MAN WILL CALL YOUR NAME TONIGHT
HE'S BEEN CALLING OH SO LONG

SOLAR

MILES DAVIS
LYRICS BY BEN SIDRAN

TIME ISN'T PASSING
IT JUST KEEPS GOING 'ROUND
KIND OF LIKE FLYING
WITH BOTH FEET ON THE GROUND
WHY SHOULD WE WORRY
WHY SHOULD WE HURRY
ON THIS WAY
WHEN NOTHING IS FOR EVER
NOTHING LASTS
BUT THE FEELING
OF REVOLVING 'ROUND THE SUN
WITHOUT FLOOR WITHOUT CEILING
WITHOUT MALICE FOR ANYONE
WHY SHOULD WE WORRY
WHY SHOULD WE HURRY
ON THIS WAY
WHEN NOTHING IS FOR EVER
NOTHING LASTS

SOLAR

SOLAR

This Miles Davis line haunted me for years and finally it demanded I write lyrics to it. I took the title as the starting point and wrote about "revolving around the sun". "Kind of like flying with both feet on the ground:" I've always wondered why, since the planet is traveling at many thousands of miles per hour as it circles around the sun and through the expanding galaxy, why we don't just fly off the surface. But of course I had to conclude with my usual admonishing: "nothing is forever and nothing lasts" – not even the sun.

SONG FOR A SUCKER LIKE YOU

BEN SIDRAN

THEY GOT A SONG FOR WINNERS
THEY GOT A SONG FOR THOSE WHO LOSE
THEY GOT A SONG FOR DEALERS
THEY GOT A SONG FOR THOSE WHO USE
THEY GOT A SONG FOR BEGGARS
THEY GOT A SONG FOR THOSE WHO CHOSE
BUT BABY
THEY DON'T HAVE A SONG FOR A SUCKER LIKE YOU

WHAT'S THAT YOU'RE SAYING
THAT YOU HAVE BEEN MISUNDERSTOOD
YOU WANT TO TAKE THE TIME TO CLEAR IT UP
MATTER OF FACT, I WISH YOU WOULD
AND IF IT'S A REAL LONG STORY, TAKE YOUR TIME
YOU CAN'T MAKE IT GOOD MAKE IT TRUE
BABY, THEY DON'T HAVE A SONG FOR A SUCKER LIKE YOU

WELL YOU GOT YOUR DOCTOR
HE'S GONNA TELL YOU HOW YOU FEEL
YOU GOT YOURSELF A LAWYER
SHE'S GONNA SHOW YOU HOW TO STEAL
NOW YOU WANT A MUSICIAN
TO MAKE YOUR DREAMS COME TRUE
BABY, THEY DON'T HAVE A SONG FOR A SUCKER LIKE YOU

SONG FOR A SUCKER LIKE YOU

I was at a party in Toronto back in 1977 when a woman came up to me and said, "Why don't you write a song for a sucker like me?" I did not know her nor do I remember her name, but I wrote this song and I continue to thank her for the suggestion.

THE SONGS OF BEN SIDRAN 1970-2020, Vol. 1

TAKE A LITTLE HIT

BEN SIDRAN

TAKE A LITTLE HIT
JUST BEFORE YOU QUIT
TAKE A LITTLE POKE
THEN YOU'LL GET THE JOKE, YOU DON'T WANNA
BUY IT BEFORE YOU TRY IT
LIFE IS WAY TOO SHORT TO MAKE THE SAME MISTAKE TWICE
SO TAKE A LITTLE HIT
BEFORE YOU

COMMIT THE OLD ROUTINE
STOP AND DIG THE SCENE
YOUR BODY AND YOUR MIND
ARE BEAUTIFULLY DESIGNED, YOU DON'T WANNA
MAX OUT THE OLD POTENTIAL FOR DROPPING THE TORRENTIAL
RAIN ON YOUR PARADE
YOU GOTTA PLAY IT WHERE IT'S LAID
WHY DON'T YOU TAKE A LITTLE HIT
BEFORE YOU QUIT

A LITTLE PULL
WHILE THE BOWL IS FULL
TOMORROW IS NEVER HERE
BUT SORROW IS EVER NEAR, YOU DONT WANNA
CANCEL THE OLD CONNECTION TO COSMIC INTROSPECTION --
WE BEEN CHEWING ON THE LEAVES AND BREWING UP THE SEEDS
SINCE THE YOUNG AND THE BRAVE WERE LIVING IN THE CAVE --
SO TAKE A LITTLE HIT
BEFORE YOU QUIT

TAKE A LITTLE TASTE
TIME IS HERE TO WASTE
TAKE A LITTLE NIP
THEN TAKE A LITTLE TRIP, IT IS NOT THE CHANCE YOU
TAKE THAT'S YOUR BIG MISTAKE, IT'S THE
CHANCE THAT YOU MISS THAT YOU SHOULDN'T RESIST
WHY DON'T YOU TAKE A LITTLE SPANK BEFORE YOU HIS THE TANK
TAKE A LITTLE STROLL BEFORE YOU HIT THE POLE
WHY DON'T YOU TAKE A LITTLE HIT
BEFORE YOU QUIT

COPYRIGHT © 2012 BEN SIDRAN
ADMINISTERED BY BULLDOG MUSIC. ALL RIGHTS RESERVED.

TAKE A LITTLE HIT

BEN SIDRAN

THANK GOD FOR THE F TRAIN

BEN SIDRAN

WHEN YOU'RE DYING ON THE PLATFORM FROM THE HEAT AND THE SMOKE
AND THE SKINNY GIRL FROM TEANECK THINKS IT'S ALL SOME KINDA JOKE
WAITING ON THE "G" TRAIN AND THE AC IS BROKE
BUT THANK GOD FOR THE F TRAIN (X2)

SOME PEOPLE RIDE TO WORK SOME PEOPLE RIDE TO WAR
SOME PEOPLE GET ON BOARD 'CAUSE THE L TRAIN'S OUT THE DOOR (IS NO MORE)
SOME PEOPLE GOT NO IDEA WHAT THEY'RE RIDING FOR
BUT THANK GOD FOR THE F TRAIN (X2)

IT MIGHT BE RAINING ON THE SURFACE, COMING DOWN IN SHEETS
FORGET THE CAR SERVICE, NOTHING'S MOVING ON THE STREETS
YOU GOTTA GET TO MID TOWN AND THERE'S NO SERVICE ON YOUR PHONE?
WELL GET YOURSELF A TICKET AND JOIN THE UNDERGROUND

LIKE THAT DRUMMER DOWN IN CHELSEA TRYING TO GET TO UNION HALL
OR THAT REAL ESTATE BROKER TRYING TO MAKE THAT CONFERENCE CALL
OR THAT GUY SELLIN' UMBRELLAS BEFORE THE PRICES FALL
THEY ALL THANK GOD FOR THE F TRAIN (X2)

THERE'S A POLITICIAN OUT HUSTLING UP SOME VOTES
THERE'S A STATISTICIAN COUNTING UP SOME GOATS
ME, I'M WONDERING WHAT THOSE TWO GIRLS ARE HIDING IN THEIR COATS
AND HERE COMES THE RIVER, YOU THINK THIS BABY FLOATS?

YOU CAN THANK OLD RONALD REAGAN FOR SCREWING UP THE SKIES
AND YOU CAN THANK THE BOYS AT NORML FOR TRYIN' TO DECRIMINALIZE
AND YOU CAN THANK THAT PLACE IN REDHOOK FOR THOSE FINE KEY-LIME PIES
BUT THANK GOD FOR THE F TRAIN (X2)

With Phil Woods.

THERE THEY GO

BEN SIDRAN

THERE THEY GO
WASN'T THAT A SWINGING SHOW
DID YOU HEAR THE FELLA SINGING
SOFT AND LOW
YOU KNOW THEY DON'T WRITE SONGS LIKE THAT ANYMORE
JUST TELLING YOU WHAT I KNOW NOW

LONG AGO
I WOULD TAKE HER TO A MOVIE SHOW
TRY TO REACH HER IN THE FEATURE
SOFT AND LOW
YOU KNOW THEY DON'T PLAY SCENES LIKE THAT ANYMORE
JUST TELLING YOU WHAT I KNOW NOW

THERE THEY GO
SAW THEM WITH MY OWN EYES
THERE THEY GO
HEARD THEM MUCH TO MY SURPRISE
THERE THEY GO THERE THEY GO THERE THEY GO
DON'T TRY TO STOP HIM'
THERE THEY GO THERE THEY GO THERE THEY GO
YOU'LL NEVER TOP HIM
THERE THEY GO THERE THEY GO THERE THEY GO

AND DON'T YOU WONDER WHERE THEY GO
WHEN IT'S TIME TO TURN THE LIGHTS DOWN LOW
DID YOU HEAR HIM ON THE ALTO SAX, HE'S BLOWING FACTS
HE'S BLOWING MYSTERIES OF LIFE I BELIEVE
PHIL WOODS BLOW ONE MORE TIME BEFORE YOU LEAVE

THERE HE GOES
SAW HIM WITH MY OWN EYES
THERE HE GOES
HEARD HIM MUCH TO MY SURPRISE
THERE HE GOES THERE HE GOES THERE HE GOES
YOU'LL NEVER TOP HIM
THERE HE GOES THERE HE GOES THERE HE GOES
YOU'LL NEVER STOP HIM
THERE HE GOES THERE HE GOES THERE HE GOES
YOU'LL NEVER MATCH HIM
THERE HE GOES THERE HE GOES THERE HE GOES
YOU'LL NEVER CATCH HIM

COPYRIGHT © 1987 BEN SIDRAN
ADMINISTERED BY BULLDOG MUSIC. ALL RIGHTS RESERVED.

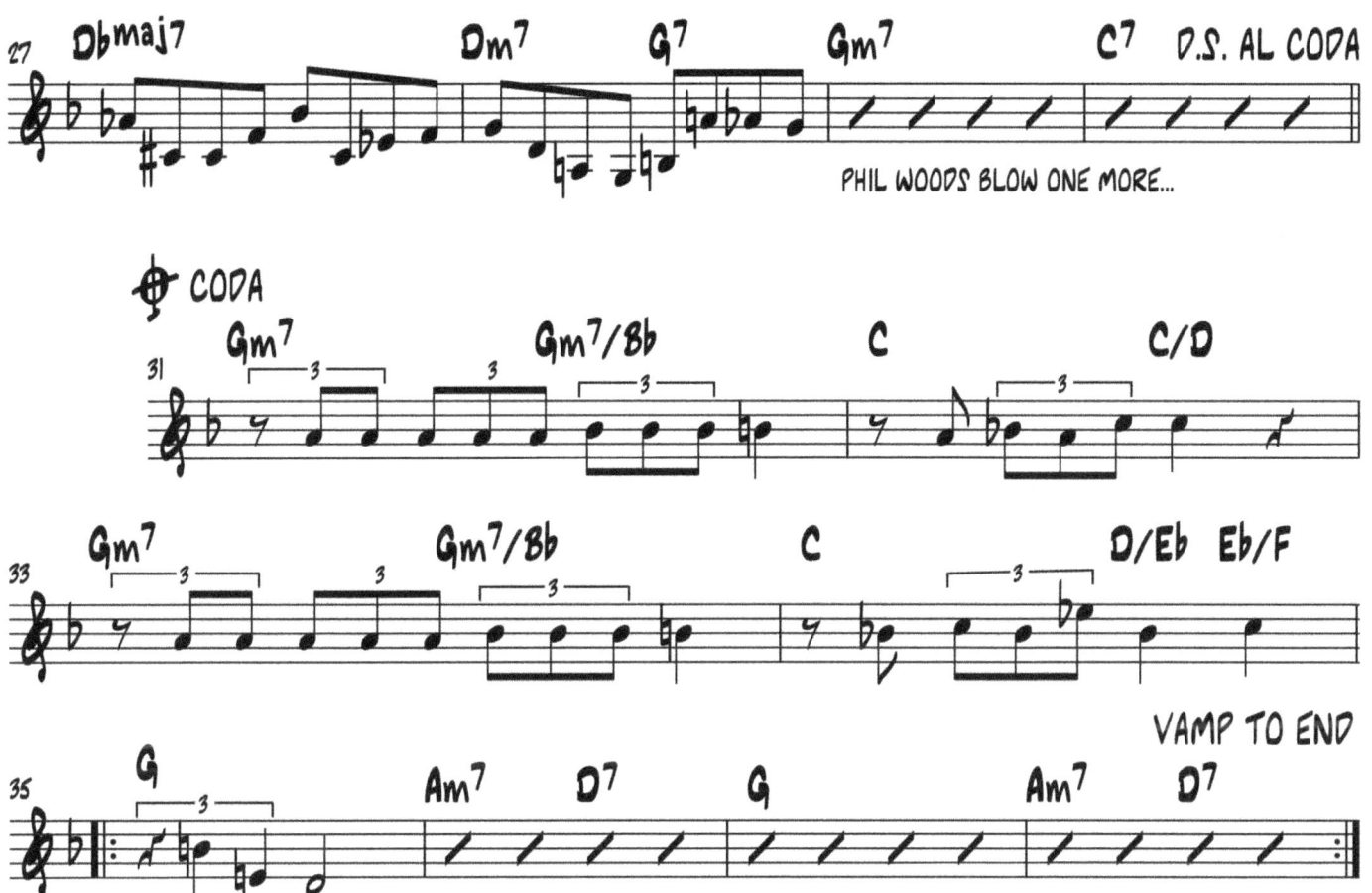

TOO HOT TO TOUCH

BEN SIDRAN

(MELODICALLY SPOKEN WORD)

I WENT TO SEE MY DOCTOR JUST TO HAVE MY FORTUNE READ
HE TOOK A LOOK, HE SHUT THE BOOK
THIS IS WHAT HE SAID
HE SAID, "YOU'RE TOO HOT TO TOUCH"
HE SAID, "YOU'RE JUST TOO HOT"
HE SAID, "I'D LIKE TO HELP YOU OUT SON BUT YOU'VE HAD TOO MUCH FUN
AND NOW YOU'RE TOO HOT, TOO HOT TO TOUCH"

SO I WENT TO SEE MY ATTORNEY, BERNIE LOOKING FOR RELIEF
HE GOT THE MAIL, HE PAID THE BAIL
HE SAID, "SON I GOT TO BE BRIEF."
HE SAID, "YOU'RE TOO HOT TO TOUCH"
HE SAID, "YOU'RE JUST TOO HOT"
HE SAID, "I'D LIKE TO HELP YOU OUT SON BUT YOU HAD TOO MUCH FUN
AND NOW YOU'RE TOO HOT TOO HOT TO TOUCH"

SO I THOUGHT MAYBE I WOULD TRAVEL
YOU KNOW HOW IT IS WHEN THE HOMETOWN FEELS A LITTLE SMALL
SOMETIMES YOU LET YOUR MIND UNRAVEL
YOU MIGHT HAVE YOURSELF A NATURAL BALL
THOUGHT I'D MOVE IT OUT EAST FIND MYSELF A BIGGER TOWN
BUT WHEN I GOT UP TO NEW YORK CITY I TRIED TO LAY MY BURDEN DOWN
THEY SAID, "UH UH.. YOU'RE JUST TOO HOT"

SO I WENT SEE MY STOCK BROKER, GOT TO FIND THE BOTTOM LINE
HE SAID "YOU JUST CAN'T KEEP CHARGIN', YOUR MARGIN'S ENLARGIN'
THIS MIGHT NOT BE YOUR TIME
HE SAID, "YOU'RE TOO HOT TO TOUCH"
HE SAID, "YOU'RE JUST TOO HOT"
HE SAID, "I'D LIKE TO HELP YOU OUT SON BUT YOU HAD TOO MUCH FUN
AND NOW YOU'RE TOO HOT TOO HOT TO TOUCH"

I THOUGHT SO...
TOO HOT, I'M TOO HOT TO TOUCH

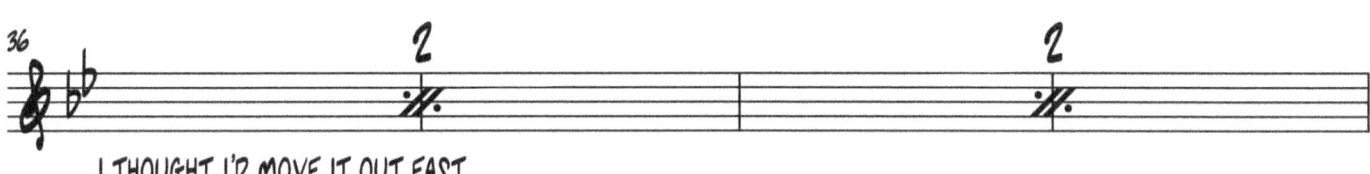

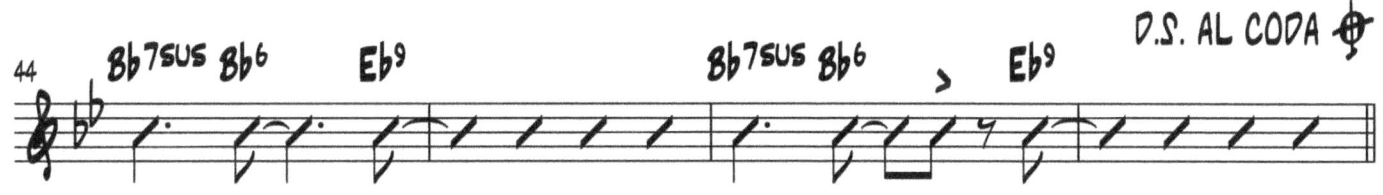
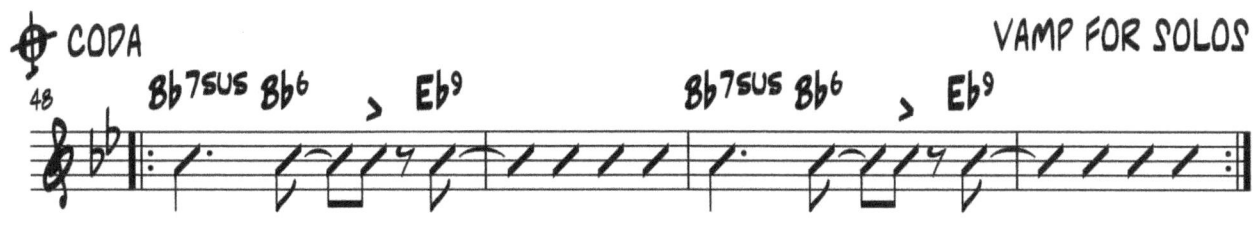

TOO MUCH TOO LATE

BEN SIDRAN

(SPOKEN WORD)

WE'RE RIDING IN A CAR THROUGH THE STREETS OF NEW ORLEANS
IT'S POURING DOWN RAIN, THE ROADS ARE NOTHING BUT STREAMS
HE'S LOOKING OUT THE WINDOW AND HE TURNS TO ME AND SAYS,
"WELCOME TO THE QUAGMIRE SON" AND THEN HE SHAKES HIS HEAD
AND SAYS SOMETHING AT THE TIME I DIDN'T REALLY UNDERSTAND
CAUSE IT CAME RIGHT OUT OF NOWHERE AND THE MAN IS SO OFFHAND,
BUT ANY TIME HE WANTS TO HE CAN CUT YOU LIKE A KNIFE.
HE SAID, "IT ALL COMES DOWN TO SOMEONE'S MONEY VERSUS SOMEONE ELSE'S LIFE."

IN A BAR IN SOHO, IT'S WINTER, AND IT'S DARK
WE'RE EATING SOME SPAGHETTI AT THIS JAZZ CLUB BY THE PARK
HE'S LAUGHING ABOUT A TIME WAY BACK IN THE PAST
AT THIS LITTLE JOINT IN TIPPO WHERE FOLKS WOULD STOP FOR GAS
PUT A NICKEL IN THE JUKE BOX AND MAKE SOME MUSIC PLAY
HAVE A COLD CO-COLA HEAR WHAT T-BONE HAD TO SAY
AND THEN HE ASKED ME, "MAN, YOU EVER HEAR ABOUT THE BO-HOG GRIND?"
I SAID, "NO," HE SAID, "ME NEITHER, MAN, BUT THAT'S WHAT I'M TRYING TO FIND."

HE SAID, "I DON'T WORRY ABOUT A THING BECAUSE NOTHING'S GONNA BE ALRIGHT"
HE SAID, "I MIGHT BE NOBODY THIS MORNING BUT I WAS SOMEBODY LAST NIGHT"
HE SAID, "I'M NOT TALKING 'CAUSE IT JUST DON'T PAY"
HE SAID, "JUST TRYING TO SWING A LITTLE IN MY WAY."

WE'RE IN A RECORDING STUDIO IN MANHATTAN, PAUL MOTIAN'S AT THE DRUMS
WE'RE TAKING A SLOW FIVE WHEN UP THIS STORY COMES
ABOUT BREW MOORE FELL DOWN THE STEPS AT TIVOLI AND DIES.
HE'S KIND OF LAUGHING BUT HE GOT THAT SAD LOOK IN HIS EYES
AND HE SAYS, "YOU KNOW THAT MAN WAS NEVER ON THE COVER OF A MAGAZINE,
AND HE JUST INHERITED A MILLION BUCKS AND THIS WAS HIS PARTING SCENE."
THERE WAS A MOMENT OF SILENCE IN RESPECT FOR MAN'S FATE
AND THEN HE SAID, "IF I EVER WRITE MY BOOK I'M GONNA CALL IT ...
TOO MUCH TOO LATE.."

HE SAID:

"IF YOU LIVE, YOUR TIME WILL COME"
"YOUR MIND IS ON VACATION BUT YOUR MOUTH IS WORKING OVERTIME"
"I DON'T HAVE NO TROUBLE LIVING, IT'S JUST DYIN' THAT BOTHERS ME"
"EVERYBODY'S CRYIN' MERCY BUT THEY DON'T KNOW THE MEANING OF THE WORD
"FOOLKILLER COMIN, GOT TO TRY TO MAKE YOUR GETAWAY."
"LOOK HERE, WHATCHA THINK YOU'RE GONNA BE DOIN' NEXT YEAR?"
"EVER SINCE THE WORLD ENDED, I DON'T GET OUT AS MUCH."
"MONEY AIN'T THE ANSER CAUSE IT CAN'T BUY CANCER."
"THAT GREY HAIRED GEEZER YOU THINK YOU SEE – THAT AIN'T ME"
"I'M JUST A LUCKY SO AND SO."
"JUST MIXING UP THE BOOGIE AND THE DO – SI – DO"
"THANK GOD FOR SELF LOVE"

TOO MUCH TOO LATE (WHAT MOSE SAID)

When I was a young man, Mose Allison's music got me through some difficult times. I was not alone; it seems that he was a light in the wilderness for a lot of folks, many of them musicians searching for a way to express themselves in the language of the blues. In time, I got the chance to produce several albums for Mose and spend time with him in New York, London, New Orleans and various other locations where musicians find shelter from the storm. He was a deep thinker, a great reader, yet a man of simple habits and dry humor. I once asked him if his lyrics were auto-biographical and he said, "Man, if I could live that life I wouldn't need to write those songs." He also said, when asked why he wasn't more famous, "Just lucky I guess." There will never be another Mose Allison. The lyrics to this song are a look back on some of the things he told me, either in person or through his recordings.

With Mose Allison, London 1995.

TURN TO THE MUSIC

BEN SIDRAN

WHEN YOUR HIGH HOPES DON'T MATERIALIZE
AND YOU'RE LOOKING AT LIFE RIGHT BETWEEN THE EYES
GOT NO GAS IN YOUR TANK, GOT NO CHICKEN IN YOUR POT
YOUR BEST FRIENDS AIN'T SO FRIENDLY NOW, AND YOUR BEST GIRL SHE AIN'T SO HOT

WHY DON'T YOU TURN TURN TURN
WHY DON'T YOU TURN TURN TURN
WHY DON'T YOU TURN, WHY DON'T YOU TURN
TURN TO THE MUSIC
YOU CAN COUNT ON THAT
TURN TO THE MUSIC
EVERY TIME

AND OUT ON THE JOB DON'T EVEN TRY TO THINK
WHEN THEY WANT YOU OPINION THEY'LL GIVE IT TO YOU NOW WATCH THE BOAT SINK
YOU'RE ADRIFT IN THE TIDE JUST ALONG FOR THE RIDE
GOT NO PLACE TO HIDE SO YOU'RE TURNING TO DRINK

WHY DON'T YOU TURN TURN TURN
WHY DON'T YOU TURN TURN TURN
WHY DON'T YOU TURN, WHY DON'T YOU TURN
TURN TO THE MUSIC
YOU CAN COUNT ON THAT
TURN TO THE MUSIC
EVERY TIME

WHEN YOUR SWEET DREAMS FINALLY COME TO PASS
THAT'S WHEN YOU NEED IT THE MOST THAT'S WHEN HEED IT THE LAST
THEY'RE ALL CALLING YOU MISTER THEY'RE ALL TALKING ABOUT YOU
NOW YOU TRY TO RESIST HER SHE KEEPS TURNING THE SCREW

WHY DON'T YOU TURN TURN TURN
WHY DON'T YOU TURN TURN TURN
WHY DON'T YOU TURN
WHY DON'T YOU TURN

WHY DON'T YOU JUST RETURN
WHY DON'T YOU TURN, WHY DON'T YOU TURN
TURN TO THE MUSIC
YOU CAN COUNT ON THAT
TURN TO THE MUSIC
EVERY TIME

COPYRIGHT © 1982 BEN SIDRAN
ADMINISTERED BY BULLDOG MUSIC. ALL RIGHTS RESERVED.

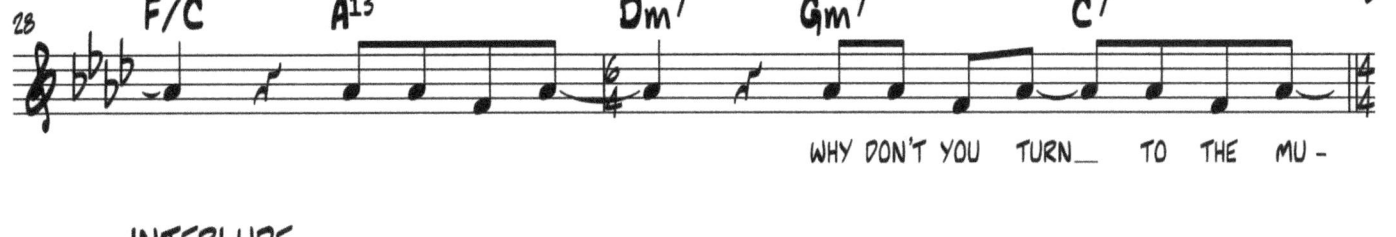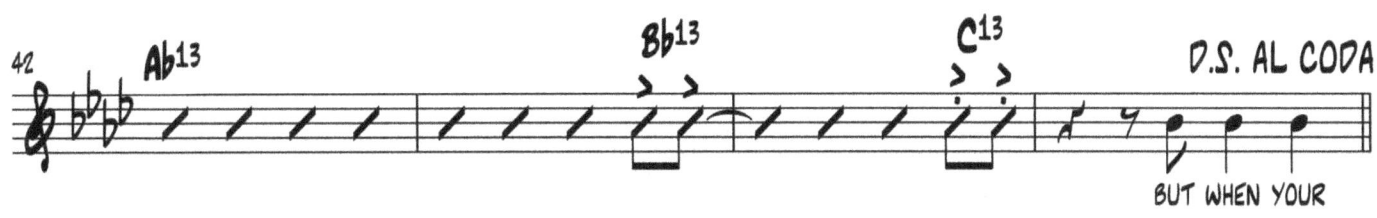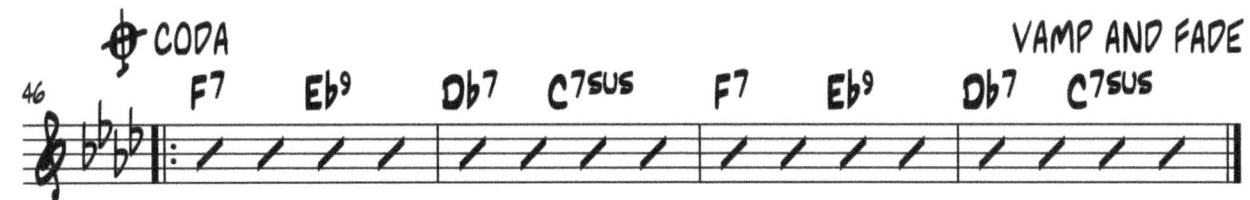

TURN TO THE MUSIC

My lyrics are generally self-evident and this is no exception. The power of music to ground us and provide relief from the ongoing assaults of life is well known and in the early 1980s, after the record business had crashed, I was thinking "forget the business, focus on the music." If you're not feeling good you're doing it wrong. You want to feel good? Listen to your favorite music.

WALKING WITH THE BLUES

BEN SIDRAN

WELL I'M WALKING
WALKING WITH THE BLUES
AND I'M TALKING
TALKING ABOUT THE BLUES
WALKING WITH THE BLUES AND
TALKING ABOUT THE BLUES
SPENDING MY LIFE
TRYING TO CHOSE THE WAY
TO GET BACK HOME
MAYBE NOT TODAY BUT THEN SOMEDAY
MAYBE NOT THIS WAY BUT MAYBE ONE WAY

THIS PLACE
AIN'T NO DISGRACE
LOTS OF PEOPLE LEARN TO LOVE
ITS FACE
LOTS OF PEOPLE LEARN
TO WATCH THE FIRES BURN
LET THEIR HAIR DOWN
GO ON INTO TOWN
BUT ME
I CAN'T GET FREE
SEEMS MY DREAMS ARE DEAD
IN THIS CITY
GOT TO HOLD ON TIGHT
HOLD ON WITH MY BARE HANDS
DON'T LET GO
DON'T LET GO OF MY RARE PLANS
DON'T THINK TWICE
ABOUT THE BAD TIMES
COLD AS ICE
SOCIAL CLIMBS
GOT TO KEEP RIGHT ON WALKING
KEEP ON TALKING
ABOUT THE BLUES

WALKING WITH THE BLUES

BEN SIDRAN

WHO'S THE OLD GUY NOW?

BEN & LEO SIDRAN

WHEN I WAS A YOUNG MAN JUST GETTING STARTED
I DIDN'T EVEN HAVE ME A RIDE INTO TOWN.
I ASKED MY HEROES OUT ON THE CORNER
I SAID NOW BROTHER, WHERE'D YOU GET THAT SOUND?

AND ONE BY ONE THE OLD MEN TOLD ME
'BOUT WHAT THEY DONE, AND SOMETIMES HOW.
WELL STEP ON UP, TAKE YOURSELF A NUMBER,
AND TAKE A LOOK AT WHO'S THE OLD GUY NOW.

TALKIN' 'BOUT BACK IN THE OLD DAYS, JUST GETTIN' STARTED
I DIDN'T EVEN HAVE ME A STORY TO TELL
NOW THAT I'M OLDER I GOT MY OWN STORY
BUT IT'S THE WAY THAT I TELL IT MAKES THE DAMN THING SELL

I BEEN LOOKIN' BACK AT ALL MY ADVENTURES
AND I'M GETTIN' TO WOND'RIN' IF THERE'S A POINT SOMEHOW.
I'M LOOKIN' FOR ANSWERS, COMIN' UP WITH NOTHIN' BUT QUESTIONS.
WELL TAKE A LOOK AT WHO'S THE OLD GUY NOW.

WHO'S THE OLD GUY NOW.
WHO'S THE OLD GUY NOW.
(VAMP TO END)

WHO'S THE OLD GUY NOW

Man, one day you wake up and look in the mirror and there's an old guy looking back at you. I like to say you never know when you're young but you will know when you're old. Actually, it's a terrific feeling knowing that one has survived so much psychic and physical combat, and the wisdom, such as it is, is hard won.

OTHER BOOKS BY BEN SIDRAN

Black Talk (DaCapo) - Black Talk examines the social function of black music in the diaspora; it sounds the depths of experience and maps the history of a culture from the jazz age to the revolutionary outbursts of the 1960s.

Talking Jazz (DaCapo) - Miles Davis, Gil Evans, Dizzy Gillespie, Jon Hendricks, Max Roach, Betty Carter, Jackie McLean, Don Cherry, Sonny Rollins, McCoy Tyner, Archie Shepp, Herbie Hancock, Tony Williams, Keith Jarrett, Wynton Marsalis, and Jack DeJohnette-these are just a few of the jazz musicians whose conversations with Ben Sidran are recorded in this volume. In stimulating, personal, and informative discussions, they not only reveal their personalities, but also detail aspects of the performance, technique, business, history, and emotions of jazz. Newly expanded with previously unpublished dialogues with David Murray, Dr. John, and Mose Allison, Talking Jazz is undoubtedly the best oral history of recent and contemporary jazz.

A Life In The Music (Taylor Trade) - Sidran's wonderfully crafted memoir revisits the many different facets of his life and career. With a charismatic and informed voice, Sidran illuminates scenes from his childhood in Chicago and gives an inside view of the recording industry, also revealing an awareness of the history of Jewish contributions to jazz.

The Ballad Of Tommy LiPuma (Nardis Books) - Tommy LiPuma was one of America's most successful record producers whose work with seminal artists like Miles Davis, Diana Krall, Barbra Streisand, Rickie Lee Jones, George Benson, and Willie Nelson went on to sell over 75 million records. Tommy's life is a picaresque journey that opens with the murder of a man on a dirt path in Sicily and concludes with five trips up the Grammy red carpet.

There Was A Fire: Jews, Music and the American Dream (Nardis Books) - A comprehensive social history of Jewish contributions to American popular music in the twentieth century. Sidran uses his first person experience to frame the story behind the story of Jews in American popular music.

CREDITS

A Is For Alligator (Blue Camus, 2014)
About Love (Feel Your Groove, 1971)
Ask Me Now (The Cat And The Hat, 1979)
At Least We Got To The Race (Don't Cry For No Hipster, 2013)
Back Nine (Don't Cry For No Hipster, 2013)
Blue Camus (Blue Camus, 2014)
Brand New Music (Don't Cry For No Hipster, 2013)
Broad Daylight (The Doctor Is In, 1977 / On The Live Side, 1986)
Chances Are (I Lead A Life, 1972)
Choice In The Matter (Get To The Point, 1984)
Critics (Too Hot To Touch, 1988)
Don't Cry For No Hipster (Don't Cry For No Hipster, 2013)
Enivre d'Amour (Too Hot To Touch, 1988)
Face Your Fears (Puttin' In Time On Planet Earth, 1973 / Life's A Lesson, 1994)
Feel Your Groove (Feel Your Groove, 1971 / Free In America, 1976)
Free In America (Free In America, 1976)
Fullness Of Time (Going Uptown - with Clementine, 2011)
Get It Yourself (The Doctor Is In, 1977)
Get To The Point (Have You Met...Barcelona - with Johnny Griffin, 1987)
Girl Talk (The Cat And The Hat, 1979)
Have You Heard The News (Puttin' In Time On Planet Earth, 1973)
I Might Be Wrong (Picture Him Happy, 2017)
I Wanna Be A Bebopper (Too Hot To Touch, 1988)
In The Beginning (Don't Cry For No Hipster, 2013)
It Didn't All Come True (Bop City, 1984)
It Don't Get No Better (Don't Cry For No Hipster, 2013)
King Of Harlem (Blue Camus, 2014)
Let's Make A Deal (Free In America, 1976)
Life's A Lesson (Life's A Lesson, 1994)
Lip Service (Cool Paradise, 1990)
Little Sherry (Bop City, 1984)
Midnight Tango (Don't Let Go, 1974)
Minority (The Cat And The Hat, 1979)
Mitsubishi Boy (On The Cool Side, 1985)
Monk's Mood (Bop City, 1984)
Nardis (Bop City, 1984)
Old Hoagy (On The Cool Side, 1985)
On The Cool Side (On The Cool Side, 1985)
Piano Players (Old Songs For The New Depression, 1982)
Picture Him Happy (Picture Him Happy, 2017)
Private Guy (Don't Cry For No Hipster, 2013)
Rich Interior Life (Don't Cry For No Hipster, 2013)
Searching For A Girl Like You (Cool Paradise, 1990)
See You On The Other Side (The Doctor Is In, 1977)
She Steps Into A Dream (Cool Paradise, 1990)
So Long (Cool Paradise, 1990)
Solar (Bop City, 1984)
Song For A Sucker Like You (The Doctor Is In, 1977)
Take A Little Hit (Don't Cry For No Hipster, 2013)
Thank God For The F Train (Picture Him Happy, 2017)
There They Go (On The Live Side, 1986)
Too Hot To Touch (Too Hot To Touch, 1988)
Too Much Too Late (Picture Him Happy, 2017)
Turn To The Music (Old Songs For The New Depression, 1982)
Walking With The Blues (Puttin' In Time On Planet Earth, 1973)
Who's The Old Guy Now (Who's The Old Guy Now, 2020)